W9-CKS-048

THE EVIL SECRET SOCIETY OF CATS

2

Story & Art By
Pandania

characters

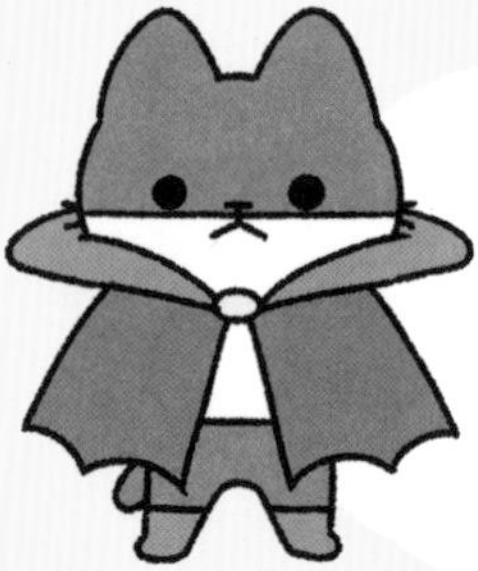

FELINE COMMANDER

Leader of the Secret Society.

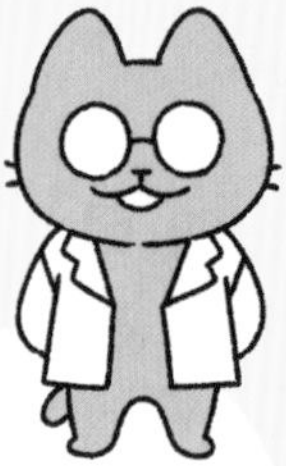

DR. MEOW

A mad scientist.

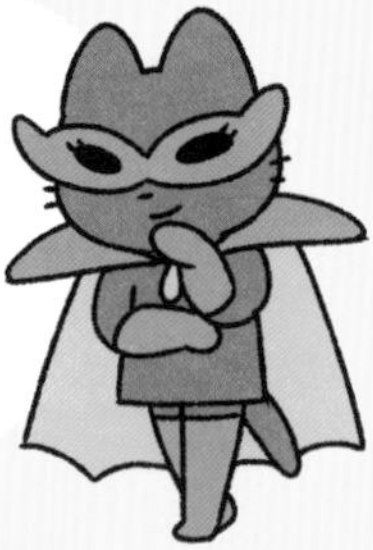

QUEEN

A brainy high-level operative.

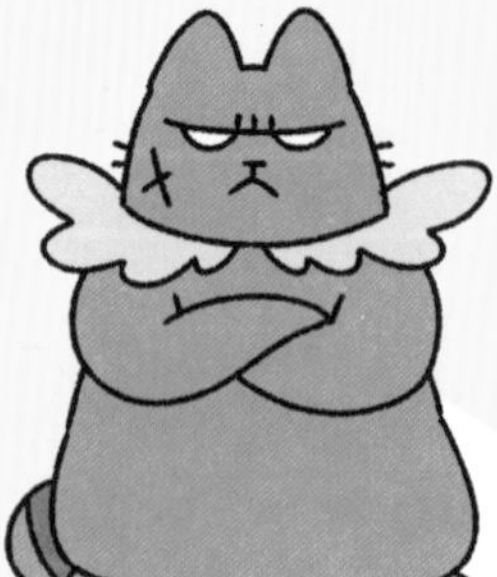

DESTROYER

The organization's muscle.

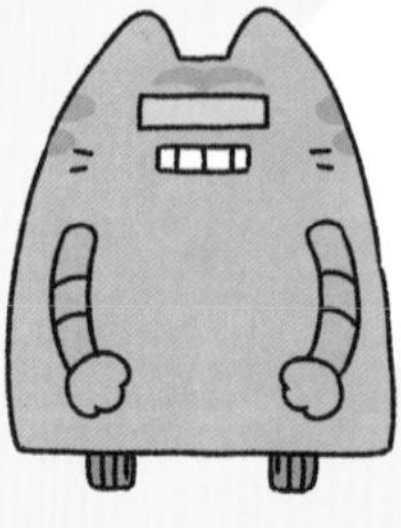

ROBOCAT

A robot created by Dr. Meow.

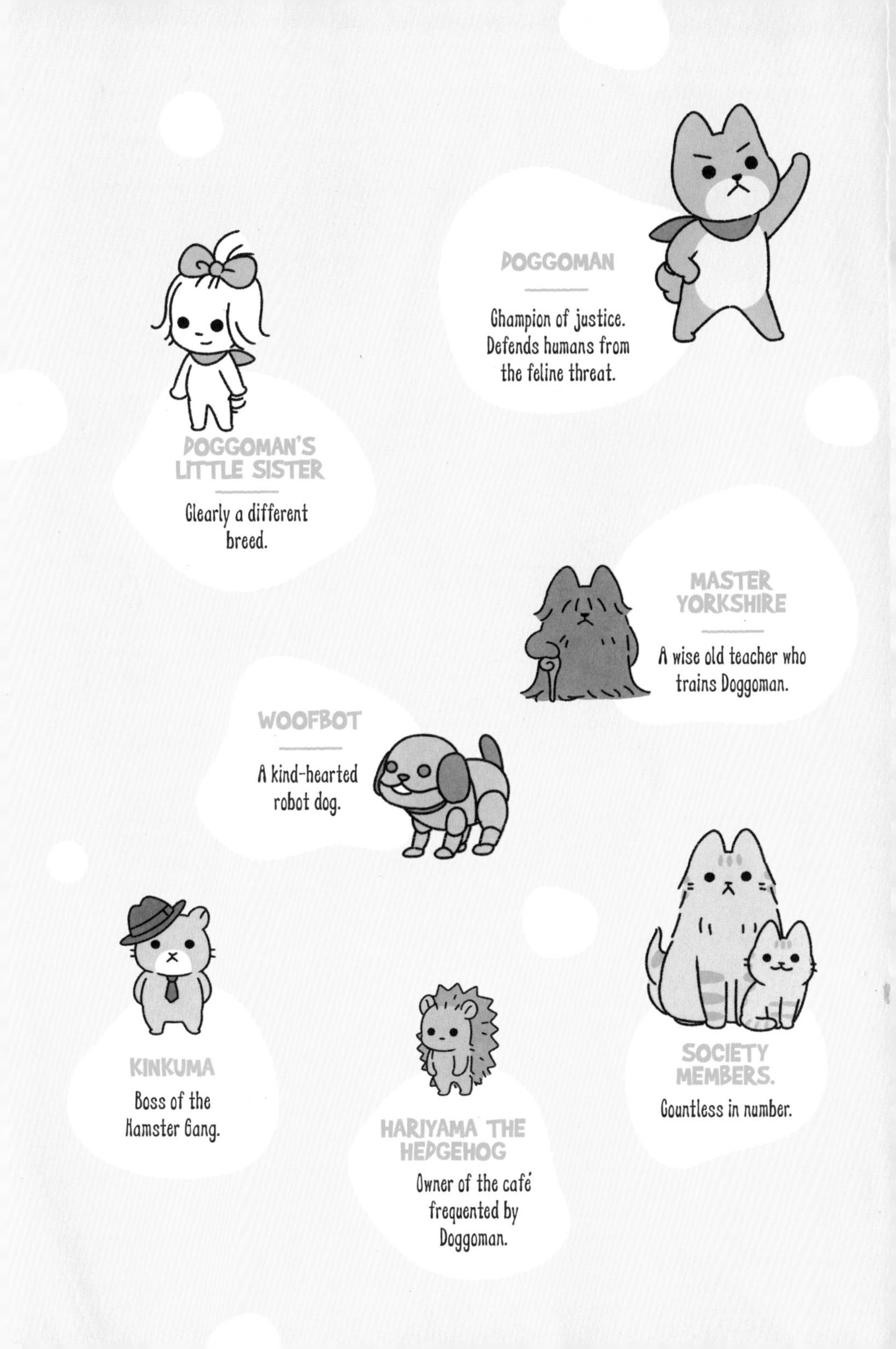
DOGGOMAN
Champion of justice. Defends humans from the feline threat.
DOGGOMAN'S LITTLE SISTER
Clearly a different breed.
MASTER YORKSHIRE
A wise old teacher who trains Doggoman.
WOOFBOT
A kind-hearted robot dog.
SOCIETY MEMBERS.
Countless in number.
HARIYAMA THE HEDGEHOG
Owner of the café frequented by Doggoman.
KINKUMA
Boss of the Hamster Gang.

Secret Society Initiative (Rewarding the Humans)

WE ARE THE EVIL SECRET SOCIETY OF CATS.

WE WILL TEACH HUMANS TO FEAR THE FELINE RACE!

THANK YOU. THAT'S SWEET, BUT... UH... WELL...

NO HUMAN IN THEIR RIGHT MIND WOULD FAIL TO APPRE- CIATE OUR GIFTS!

Hariyama: ... (I went through a lot in my youth. But none of that is worth mentioning now. I only watch over the futures of our young ones. I believe that is where hope lies.)

Society Members' Secret Training

SHE GETS SO INTO IT!
DO YOU THINK CATS FORGET THAT IT'S THEIR OWN TAIL?
LITTLE DO THE HUMANS KNOW...
THAT SOCIETY MEMBERS NEVER MISS A DAY OF PERSONAL TRAINING.
Heart, Technique, Physique, Cat Food
ONE SIMPLE TRAINING TECHNIQUE IS TO SEE YOUR TAIL AS THE ENEMY.

Destroyer: Often trains at the neighborhood Shinto shrine. Queen: Never misses a day of fitness training. Dr. Meow: Wants to upload his consciousness into cyberspace.

Dr. Meow's Favorite Pastime

THE FLAVOR OF THIS FOOD HAS DE-CREASED IN QUALITY.
IT DIS-PLEASES ME.
I'VE HAD THE MINIONS REPLACE YOUR FOOD.
FUR-COVERE
OH! THIS IS DELICIOUS! I'LL ONLY EAT THIS FROM NOW ON.
AND ALL I DID WAS PUT THE OLD FOOD ON A NEW DISH!
HEH HEH...

Doggoman: I get antsy patrolling on days when I'm going to get my favorite food, but a hero must be patient!

Doggoman's Little Sister: My brother's been antsy all day.

Tremble! The Commander's Song

THE WIND FEELS LOVELY.
ONE CAN'T HELP SINGING ON A DAY LIKE THIS.
OOOHH TO OUR GREAT-NESS, THE GREAT-NESS OF CATS!
DID YOU HEAR A CAT YOWLING?
I TOTAL-LY DID!
DO YOU THINK THERE'S A CAT FIGHT NEARBY?

Feline Commander: *Oh, to our greatness, the greatness of cats. Raise your tails up to the sky, now is the time for our meows to ring out. Once we gather 'round the treats, the world will dance on the pads of our paws. O cats, o cats, o cats.* (First verse.)

Robocat vs. Feline Commander

I'M SLEEPY... TIME FOR A NAP.
ZZZ. ZZZ.
HEY, ROBO-CAT! GET UP!
AT LEAST MAKE ROOM FOR ME!

Feline Commander: *Oh, to our greatness, the greatness of cats. Dig your claws into the screen doors, now is the time for our meows to ring out. Once we gather 'round the catnip, the world will be buried in our belly fur. O cats, o cats, o cats.* (Second verse.)

Secret Society Initiative (Enchantment in the Streets--Cat Statues)

WE ARE THE EVIL SECRET SOCIETY OF CATS.
OH, LOOK. A CAT.
WE WILL TEACH HUMANS TO FEAR THE FELINE RACE!
WHAT A PRETTY ORANGE TABBY.
IS IT A BOY OR A GIRL? I WONDER HOW OLD IT IS. IT LOOKS YOUNG.
Welcome
Neko osteopathy
IT WAS JUST A STATUE.
KEEP FALLING FOR THIS DECEPTION, HUMAN!
SKFF SKFF

Feline Commander: I wrote the Society's anthem lyrics, and the Doctor wrote the melody. There are twenty verses, but no one knows more than the first two.

Doggoman Awakens

I DIDN'T EVEN GET TO SAY GOODBYE.

I WILL WANDER THE TOWN IN SEARCH OF YOUR WARMTH.

I ASK MYSELF AGAIN AND AGAIN-- WHY?

BUT THERE IS NO ANSWER, AND SO I TURN MY EYES AHEAD.

SO GOES THE SOLITARY HERO'S LULLABY. (AH....)

HIS FAVORITE BLANKET WAS THROWN AWAY.

ON THIS DAY, DOGGOMAN TOOK ONE STEP CLOSER TO ADULTHOOD.

Doggoman: Spent a long while staring at the place where his blanket used to be.

Doggoman's Little Sister: He'll recover. He just needs time.

11

Meeting of Evil Leaders

IT'S TIME.
I'M READY.
THEN ALL WE NEED IS DR. MEOW.
MY PREPARATIONS ARE COMPLETE.
WELL DONE, DOCTOR.
ONCE A YEAR, THE EVIL LEADERS MEET IN SECRET...
TO PLAN FELINE COMMANDER'S SURPRISE BIRTHDAY PARTY.

Feline Commander: I never told anyone in the Society—not even the leaders—when my birthday is, but at some point the Doctor found out.

Secret Society Initiative (Stripped of Your Freedom to Sleep)

WE ARE THE EVIL SECRET SOCIETY OF CATS.
WOW, YOU'RE HYPER.
THUNDER THUNDER THUNDER
WE WILL TEACH HUMANS TO FEAR THE FELINE RACE!
YOU USED TO RUN AROUND ALL NIGHT WHEN YOU WERE A KITTEN.
I'M SO GLAD YOU DON'T DO THAT ANYMORE.
OF COURSE, YOU **DO** WAKE ME UP AT FOUR IN THE MORN-ING...
WE WILL DICTATE THE HOURS IN WHICH YOU SLEEP!

Robocat: Has a timer function, allowing it to set its active hours, but no one knows about this so it never gets used. When the Commander tries to wake Robocat, it ignores him.

Secret Society Initiative (The Melody of Despair!)

WE ARE THE EVIL SECRET SOCIETY OF CATS.
LOOK! A CUTE SCRATCHING POST!
WE WILL TEACH HUMANS TO FEAR THE FELINE RACE!
HERE. USE THIS.
SCRITCH
SCRITCH
SCRATCH
YES! DRINK IN THE SYMPHONY OF DESTRUCTION!
SCRATCH
SCRATCH
SCRATCH
SCRATCH
SCRATCH
CAT LOVER

Dr. Meow: The Society member most sensitive to heat and cold. Has been yelled at by Feline Commander for abusing the A/C.

Master Yorkshire's Past

CREAK
OKOHAMA
OG PARK
IT HAPPENED BACK WHEN I WAS TRAINING TO BE A WARRIOR...
Well. Haven't seen *your* face 'round here.
Heh. Maybe we'll *ruff* you up a little.
THEN I UN-LEASHED MY CHI ENERGY, AND...
Excellent. I was just getting bored.
FWOOM
WHAT HAPPENED NEXT, MASTER?!
No balls at the park
...

Doggoman: I want to go on a journey where I train to be a warrior like my master did!

Doggoman's Little Sister: (I don't want him to go too far...)

Queen's Schemes (Remote Work Thirst Traps)

SO, IF YOU CAN REVISE ALL THAT DATA BY THE END OF TOMORROW ...?
I THINK I CAN GET IT DONE BY THEN.
GREAT! CAN'T WAIT TO SEE IT.
DO YOU HAVE ANY OTHER QUES-TIONS FOR ME?
YES. "CAN I SEE YOUR CAT?"
NO, THAT SHOULD DO IT.
THIS IS A THIRST TRAP.

Queen: Primarily a strategist but is also agile and highly athletic. She's especially good at climbing up to high places.

Record of One Man's Transformation

MY FATHER WAS ALWAYS VERY SERIOUS ABOUT PROPER LAN-GUAGE.
AND THEN, JUST A SPRINKLE OF GARVIN-MAYO*!
Why do people have to use all those cutesy abbrevi-ations?
BUT LATE-LY...
YOU'RE A GOOD KITTY, CHATARO.
YOU'RE AS CUTE AS EVER.
THERE, THERE! YOU'RE TOTES ADORBS, CHATA-CHAN.
CHATA-CHAN, CHII-CHAN, ADORACHII-CHAN~!
OUR MYSTERI-OUS POWER HAS UNDONE YOUR FATHER'S CONVIC-TIONS.

The TV girl is talking about garlic-ponzu vinegar mayonnaise.

Dr. Meow: Likes interesting things. Destroyer: Is more caring than he looks. Feline Commander: Can be sensitive, but as usual, refuses to admit it.

Secret Society Initiative (A New Base)

WE ARE THE EVIL SECRET SOCIETY OF CATS.
Five years ago.
I hope you like your new home.
WE WILL TEACH HUMANS TO FEAR THE FELINE RACE!
Now, play nice.
Three years ago.
Two years ago.
THIS HOUSE IS NOW A BASE OF OPERA-TIONS FOR US!
Today.

Hariyama: (I visit cafés on my days off. Lately I go to the Tanuki-san place. It's in a thicket far away from any residential areas, so it may not be easy for humans to find it.)

Destroyer's Training (Aim for the Heights!)

UGH, WHY MUST YOU GUYS CLIMB THE CURTAINS?
WHY DO WE CLIMB THE CURTAINS? BECAUSE THEY'RE THERE.
AIM FOR THE DISTANT SUMMIT. THIS IS THE WAY OF THE CURTAIN.

Destroyer: There are 108 paths to master in felinedom. Even I have not mastered them all.

Slow Day at the Society

I HAVE COMPLETED THE PERFECT CAT WAND! GUARANTEED TO ENTRANCE ANY CAT!
REALLY? ANY CAT? THAT'S HARD TO BELIEVE.
...
MUST BE A SLOW DAY.
YES.

Destroyer: The Doctor was already in the Society when I joined. Queen: When I first met him, the Doctor was riding a giant robot vacuum cleaner.

Doggoman and Doggoman's Little Sister Go to the Beach (Part 1)

DOG-GOMAN AND HIS LITTLE SISTER HAVE BEEN TAKEN TO THE BEACH.

ZZSHHH
ZZSHHH

THE OCEAN SURE IS BIG!

Doggoman: His tail occasionally droops when he remembers sharing a treat with his sister and taking the bigger piece.

Doggoman's Little Sister: She adores sharing treats with Doggoman.

22

Doggoman and Doggoman's Little Sister Go to the Beach (Part 2)

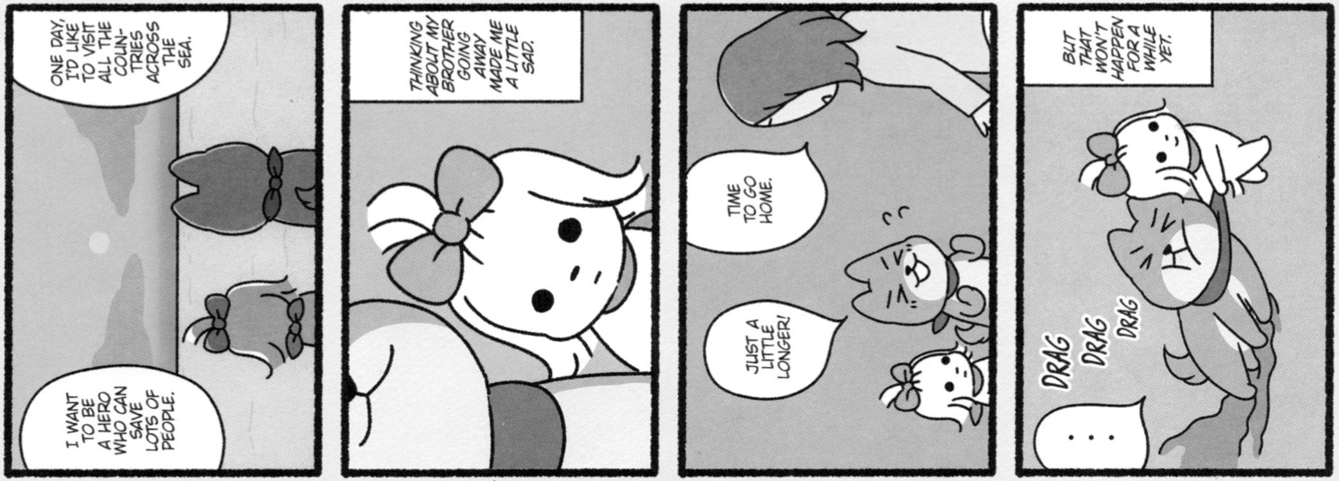
ONE DAY, I'D LIKE TO VISIT ALL THE COUN-TRIES ACROSS THE SEA.
I WANT TO BE A HERO WHO CAN SAVE LOTS OF PEOPLE.
THINKING ABOUT MY BROTHER GOING AWAY MADE ME A LITTLE SAD.
TIME TO GO HOME.
JUST A LITTLE LONGER!
BUT THAT WON'T HAPPEN FOR A WHILE YET.
DRAG
DRAG
DRAG
. . .

Doggoman: I got to play at the beach! It was so much fun! Doggoman's Little Sister: There were so many new smells at the beach.

Destroyer's Human Training (Raise Your Concentration)

YES!
THIS IS HOW WE TRAIN THE HUMANS IN CONCENTRATION.

Destroyer: They say the wings he wears on his shoulders are a trophy he stole from a giant monster bird, but the truth remains unclear.

A Day in the Life of Robocat (Part 1)

THE CAT AT KANA-CHAN'S HOUSE IS SO CUTE! I WISH I COULD HAVE A CAT.
MY DAUGHTER WON'T STOP TALKING ABOUT IT.
OH, YOU MEAN TORAEMON.
WHAT KIND OF CAT IS IT?
UM, WELL, IT'S A BIG TABBY WE FOUND ABANDONED ON THE STREET.
ALL TECHNICALLY TRUE.

Dr. Meow: Does maintenance on Robocat whenever it comes back to the base. Occasionally makes minor upgrades.

Robocat: Version 1.3.5. Minor bug fixes.

A Day in the Life of Robocat (Part 2)

YIKES!
PHEW! JUST A CAT.
HUH?
VMMM
TORAEMON!
HI, DADDY!
MEOW.

Robocat: Generally has no smell, but sometimes a unique odor will come from its mouth region.

Grandmother's Secret (Legacy Society Membership)

I'M NOT GETTING ANY YOUNGER.
OH, GRAND-MA...
IF ANY-THING HAPPENS TO ME, TAKE CARE OF MIKEKO.
OH, AND TAKE THIS.
A SECRET SOCIETY?
SMIRK
THAT'S WHEN I LEARNED THAT MY GRAND-MOTHER WAS IN THE EVIL SECRET SOCIETY OF CATS.

Feline Commander: Records TV programs (aimed at cats) but forgets to watch them. Doggoman: Completely forgets to watch a show he's been looking forward to for days.

Secret Society Initiative (Creating an Inertial Nightmare)

WE ARE THE EVIL SECRET SOCIETY OF CATS.
I NEED TO GET GOING SOON.
WE WILL TEACH HUMANS TO FEAR THE FELINE RACE!
AWWW, BUT I CAN'T MOVE, CAN I?!
MOOSH MOOSH
I REALLY HAVE TO RUN AN ERRAND.
AWW, HOW AM I SUPPOSED TO MOVE NOW?!
Gray Tabby
THAT ERRAND WILL NEVER GET DONE! EVER!

Queen: Wants a feline hot spring at the base, but the Commander is against it.

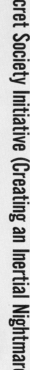

Secret Society Initiative (No Outfit Is Complete Without a Cat's Touch)

WE ARE THE EVIL SECRET SOCIETY OF CATS.
WE WILL TEACH HUMANS TO FEAR THE FELINE RACE!
I JUST BOUGHT THIS AND ITS ALREADY HAIRED UP!
PERFECT FIT.
KAN
OW! OW!
KAN
SCRATCH
SCRATCH
WE WILL ADD THE FINISH-ING TOUCH TO YOUR ENSEM-BLES!

Feline Commander: No one has seen him out of uniform. Dr. Meow: Always wears a white lab coat.

Evacuating Society Members

THE SOCIETY HAS A SPECIAL SATEL-LITE FOR TRACKING THE WEATHER.
WHEN TY-PHOONS OR OTHER BIG STORMS STRIKE, ALL MEM-BERS ARE EVACU-ATED TO THE BASE.

Robocat: It clearly consumes more fuel than it expends. What it does with that extra energy is unknown.

Secret Society Initiative (Shocking Game Disruption Technique)

WE ARE THE EVIL SECRET SOCIETY OF CATS.
WE WILL TEACH HUMANS TO FEAR THE FELINE RACE!
Shoot! It was just getting good!
THAT USED TO HAPPEN ALL THE TIME...
AND IT STILL DOES.
DU-DUN
BEHOLD OUR MAD SKILLZ THAT CLEAR EVERY LEVEL!

Feline Commander: Wants people to think he's good at tactical games. Dr. Meow: Disappears when his favorite games go on sale. Destroyer: Good at (physical) games.

Evil Lurks in the Shadows

THE CAT SOCIETY'S BEEN AWFULLY QUIET LATELY.
A LITTLE *TOO* QUIET...
HEH HEH... EVIL IS A THING THAT LURKS IN THE SHADOWS.
MIIIN
MIIIN
MIIIN
ON HOT DAYS, FELINE COM-MANDER NEVER LEAVES THE SHADE.

Doggoman: My favorite season is summer. But I get super excited in the spring, the sky is so pretty in winter, and autumn walks are lots of fun!

The Doctor's Business (Cat Yoga Class)

I'VE BEEN ACHING ALL OVER LATELY.
I KNOW A PLACE THAT'LL HELP YOU OUT.
THIS SEEMS KINDA SHADY...
SECRET
TWO PLEASE, SENSEI.
VERY WELL, PUT THESE ON.
IT'S WORKING!
THIS IS THE CAT POSE.
ISN'T IT GREAT?!

Dr. Meow: Rumor has it he once lost to a cicada. He denies it.

A Day in the Life of Destroyer

LOOK, SHIMAO-CHAN. I GOT YOU A NEW BRUSH.
THE SALES-PERSON SAID IT'S VERY GOOD.
GLEAM
GLIMMER
WHERE IS DES-TROYER?
HE SAYS HE'S UNABLE TO ATTEND.
DES-TROYER DIDN'T SHOW HIMSELF FOR A WHILE.

Destroyer: Actually is somewhat long-haired, which is why he looks smaller when he gets out of the bath.

Secret Society Initiative (Overwriting Standards of Cuteness)

WE ARE THE EVIL SECRET SOCIETY OF CATS.
BAKERY
WE WILL TEACH HUMANS TO FEAR THE FELINE RACE!
THIS BREAD IS SO CUTE. IT LOOKS LIKE CAT PAWS.
THIS SHOULDER BAG IS CUTE. IT LOOKS LIKE A CALICO CAT.
THAT CLOUD IS SO CUTE. IT LOOKS LIKE A CAT.
WE'VE PRO-GRAMMED HER TO SEE US AS THE STANDARD FOR CUTENESS!

Feline Commander: Always wears gloves, but apparently his paws feel delightful. Rumor has it they're the softest in the Society.

Dr. Meow's Business (Translation App)

DR. MEOW HAS SECRETLY DEVELOPED A CAT TRANSLATION APP.
MEOW!
Fun socks are good weather
"FUN SOCKS ARE GOOD WEATHER"?
WHAT THE HECK? THAT'S SO FUNNY.
IT MAKES NO SENSE.
SMIRK
I DELIBERATELY MADE THE ACCURACY LOW.
WE CAN'T LET THEM LEARN OUR SECRETS, AFTER ALL.
Neco Cola

Feline Commander: For a time, plastic bottles were our arch nemesis, but we have developed a plan to counter them.

Grandmother's Secret (The Truth About Member Activity)

WHAT DO ELITE MEM-BERS DO?
OH, NOTHING SPECIAL.
WE CHAT WITH OTHER MEM-BERS.
I THOUGHT THOSE WERE YOUR TEA BUDDIES.
WE HELP INJURED CATS AND FIND THEM HOMES.
I THOUGHT YOU JUST LIKED FOSTERING CATS.
SOME-TIMES WE GET ORDERS FROM THE FELINE COM-MAND-ER.
MIND YOUR HEALTH.
WHO ?!

Feline Commander: Regularly gives direct orders to the highest-level Society members. The contents of these orders are shrouded in mystery.

Queen's Evil Plot (Surprise Doppelgänger?)

MEOW!
HUH? WHEN DID YOU GET OUT?!
HOLD ON, I'LL LET YOU IN!
MEOW.
HUH?
OH, IT WAS A LOOK-ALIKE!
HEE HEE. SUR-PRISED YOU, DIDN'T WE, HUMAN?

Queen: Treads quietly. Destroyer: Treads loudly. Feline Commander: Treads normally. Dr. Meow: Sometimes makes mysterious noises.

Wallpaper Art Exhibition

THE SOCIETY HOLDS A WALL-PAPER ART CONTEST ONCE A YEAR.
IT DIS-PLAYS WORKS FROM ALL OVER THE COUN-TRY.

Destroyer: He's concerned that the rumors about him are getting overblown: he battled a lion, he beat a pack of tigers with just his tail, he swung an elephant by its trunk and sent it flying, etc. etc.

Doggoman's Shocking Encounter (Part 1)

WOOF.
OOFBOT 3
A MECHA HERO! WHAT'S YOUR NAME?!
I'M DOGGO-MAN!
THAT DAY, DOGGO-MAN HAD A SHOCK-ING EN-COUNTER.

Doggoman: Is gradually coming to love his new blanket. Doggoman's Little Sister: Likes the pattern on the new blanket.

Doggoman's Shocking Encounter (Part 2)

SO, YOUR NAME IS WOOF-BOT!
WOOF!
AND YOU'RE A HERO THAT PROTECTS HUMANS IN THEIR HOMES!
WOOF!
WE CAN BE HEROES TOGETHER!
SEE YOU TOMORROW!
WOOF!

Doggoman: Prefers a fluffy blanket to a smooth one. Likes to hug it while sleeping.

Doggoman's Shocking Encounter (Part 3)

THE NEXT DAY.
Stand on this machine for full-body toning!
Give it a try!
SORRY, YESTERDAY WAS WOOFBOT'S LAST DAY ON DISPLAY.
I'M SURE YOU'LL SEE WOOFBOT AGAIN.
YEAH...
ONWARD, DOGGO-MAN! BELIEVE YOU'LL HAVE A REUNION WITH YOUR FRIEND!

Hariyama: ... (Looking at the sunset reminds me of the old days. Back when I had just started running the café, [an hour's worth of reminiscences abridged] and it's etched in my memory to this day.)

Secret Society Initiative (Update on the Tanaka Home Brainwashing)

WE ARE THE EVIL SECRET SOCIETY OF CATS.
MY FATHER'S CHANGED.
WE WILL TEACH HUMANS TO FEAR THE FELINE RACE!
FIRST, HE STARTED BURSTING INTO TEARS JUST FROM SEEING A CAT ON TV.
NOW HE CRIES AT EVERY LITTLE THING.
CHATARO... THANK YOU FOR BEING BORN.
CATS TRANS-FORM HUMANS. IT'S IRRE-VERSIBLE!
ZZZ ZZZ

Queen: Takes good care of her fur and claws but has no interest in the Doctor's beauty products. Dr. Meow: Will never reveal his secret ingredients.

The Tanaka Family Secret

WHAT'S COME OVER DAD LATELY?
OH, SWEETIE. TAKE A LOOK AT THIS.
Our Wedding
HE WAS CRYING ALL THE TIME WHEN YOU WERE BORN, TOO.
HE'S *ALWAYS* BEEN LIKE THAT.
RIIIGHT...

Feline Commander: Our current focus is how to deal with sneaky cucumbers.

Master Yorkshire's Past (Part 2)

THIS HAPPENED WHEN I WAS YOUNG.
You'll come back, won't you?
...
I never make promises.
Pet Salon: Kosugi
I am a ship. I go where the wind takes me.
AND SO, I PUT THE SALON BEHIND ME.
SO... SO GROWN-UP.

Doggoman's Little Sister: My brother has so much respect for his master.

Tremble Before the Secret Society's Highest-Level Members!

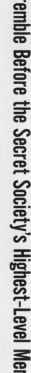

DID YOU HEAR THAT CAT?
HEH... SO NAÏVE.
THAT WAS CHILDREN PLAYING.
WHEE!
AH HA HA HA HA!
BICYCLE BRAKES AND CRYING BABIES SOUND LIKE CATS, TOO. SO BE CAREFUL.
THESE ELITE SOCIETY MEMBERS NEVER FAIL TO IMPRESS ME.

Destroyer: Trains Society members at their dojo a few times a week. This week's goals are overcoming the vacuum cleaner and one-hit TV KO.

Doggoman's Little Sister's Dilemma

MY BROTHER STILL DOESN'T KNOW.
....
WHAT WILL YOU DO ABOUT IT?
I... I DON'T KNOW.
I DON'T WANT TO CRUSH HIS DREAMS.
OH BOY! SANTA'S COMING!
DOGGOMAN'S LITTLE SISTER COULDN'T TELL HIM THAT "SANTA CLAUS" IS THEIR OWNER.

Doggoman: I want to meet Santa!

Doggoman's Little Sister: I don't need any gifts.

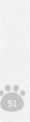

Secret Society Initiative (Christmas Eve Tree-Trouncing Party)

WE ARE THE EVIL SECRET SOCIETY OF CATS.
WE WILL TEACH HUMANS TO FEAR THE FELINE RACE!
LET THE PARTY BEGIN!

Feline Commander: If Santa Claus is real, I would like a new chair (Robocat broke mine). Destroyer: A driver's license. Dr. Meow: A moon base. Queen: That's a secret.

Elite Member Report (Elite Member Negligence)

WE ARE THE EVIL SECRET SOCIETY OF CATS.
PLEASE, FORGIVE ME!
TODAY WE CHECK IN ON ONE OF OUR ELITE HUMAN MEMBERS.
I WASN'T PLANNING TO DO IT! I JUST COULDN'T SAY NO!
I WON'T GO TO A CAT CAFÉ WITHOUT TELLING YOU EVER AGAIN!
I SAID I'M SORRYYY!
WE SHOW NO MERCY EVEN TO OUR MOST ELITE MEMBERS!

Queen: Slightly older than the Commander. Destroyer: Slightly older than the Commander. Dr. Meow: Age unknown. Robocat: A kitten.

The Commander and the Doctor

DIDN'T I SAY YOU CAN'T BE UP THERE?
ARE YOU EVEN LISTEN-ING?
I TOLD YOU TO ASK FOR PERMIS-SION BEFORE INVENT-ING NEW THINGS!
TIME FOR BRUSH-ING.
BEEEEEP
TIME FOR BRUSH-ING.
BEEEEEP
ARE YOU EVEN LISTEN-ING?!

Dr. Meow: After this, a strange new invention wandered into the Commander's private quarters and went berserk. A few minutes later, it exploded, causing heavy damage.

Destroyer's Training (Mastering the Cat Door)

HAVING MASTERED THE WAY OF THE CAT DOOR...

DESTROYER CAN NOW SQUEEZE THROUGH THE SMALLEST ONE.

Destroyer: Isn't afraid of water and likes baths. Also meditates under waterfalls.

Feline Commander: I fear no bath!

Dr. Meow: Heh heh.

The Mystery of Queen

SOCIETY LEADER QUEEN...

IS ALSO COCO, THE FELINE SENSATION OF ADS AND TV DRAMAS.

Coco-chan Calendar Reserve yours today

BUT NO ONE IN THE SOCIETY HAS REALIZED THIS.

HAA, I'M TIRED. I WANT SOME YAKINIKU.

SEE ME, MY CAT, AND YAKINIKU, IN THEATERS NOW.

AND, OF COURSE, DOG-GOMAN DOESN'T KNOW, EITHER.

Feline Commander: What in the world was that berserk invention? I completely fail to see the point, not to mention the expense. Dr. Meow: Munch munch.

Operation: Cattify the Snow People

COOL, A SNOW-MAN WITH CAT EARS!
THERE'S ANOTHER ONE.
WHAT? THESE, TOO?!
THE PREVIOUS NIGHT, THE SOCIETY LAUNCHED ITS LARGEST OPERA-TION YET: ADDING CAT EARS TO EVERY SNOWMAN IN TOWN.

Doggoman: The first time I saw snow I was surprised, then so happy I got the zoomies!

Doggoman's Little Sister: Yesterday, my brother dove head-first into a pile of snow. He'll jump into piles of leaves, too.

Queen's Schemes (Making Light Sport)

YOU IGNORED ME A MINUTE AGO.
BUT NOW YOU'RE ALL NEEDY.
AWWW, IT'S CUTE HOW FICKLE YOU ARE!
HUMANS REALLY ARE ADOR-ABLE, AREN'T THEY?
MEOW.

Queen: Sometimes wakes up the Commander, who curls up under the blankets when it's cold. The Doctor cleverly hides himself to avoid being woken. Dr. Meow: (They always find him in the end.)

Queen's Stratagem (Humans as Playthings)

KICK
KICK
LICK
LICK
CHOMP
CHOMP
HUMANS ARE A CAT'S PLAY-THINGS.

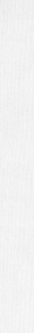

Doggoman's Little Sister: Sometimes gets complimented by a stranger and clams up because she doesn't know what to say.

The Doctor's Favorite Pastime: Bear Power Headgear (Cat Hoods)

COM-MANDER, I'VE DEVELOPED A NEW WEAPON.
OHO?
WHAT IS THIS?
IT GIVES YOU THE BRUTE STRENGTH OF A BEAR.
IT'S TRUE! IN-CRED-IBLE!
SNAP SNAP

Feline Commander: Insists that he does not believe in fortune-telling. Doggomar: Is always curious about the fortune-telling segments of TV shows.

A Day in the Life of Destroyer (Tomorrow It Will Be Me)

BUT DID IT REALLY HAVE TO LOOK LIKE *THIS?*
SNAP
SNAP
THE SHAPE IS BASED ON FELINE ENGI-NEERING.
POOR COM-MANDER.
WELCOME BACK, SHIMAO-CHAN.
I'M KNITTING SOME-THING JUST FOR YOU.
Handmade Kitty Hood

Destroyer: Sometimes it's like she still thinks I'm a kitten.

Destroyer's Training (Empty Your Mind)

CLAW CLIPPING, BABIES, BRUSHING.
IF YOU CAN EMPTY YOUR MIND, YOU CAN ENDURE THEM ALL.

Destroyer: Something happened recently that required him to empty his mind.

Secret Society Initiative (Winter's Harbinger, Thy Name Is Cat)

WE ARE THE EVIL SECRET SOCIETY OF CATS.
THE KOTATSU'S OUT!
WE WILL TEACH HUMANS TO FEAR THE FELINE RACE!
YAY! I'LL JUST SLIDE RIGHT UNDER...
OOPS, SORRY.
BONK
OW! OW! I SAID I WAS SORRY!
TASTE THE PAIN THAT WINTER BRINGS!

Feline Commander: We cats learned to overcome the cold long ago! (He insists.) Doggoman: Heroes don't mind the cold! (He insists.)

Secret Society Initiative (Grand Champions of Bed Sumo)

WE ARE THE EVIL SECRET SOCIETY OF CATS.

NIGHTY-NIGHT!

WE WILL TEACH HUMANS TO FEAR THE FELINE RACE!

SHE'S OUT OF THE RING! THE CAT WINS!

Feline Commander: A lightweight in cat sumo but has a reputation for speed. Sometimes gets careless when trying to do special moves.

Destroyer: Was the undefeated champion of cat sumo, but recently a new rival has appeared (Robocat).

Notes from a Young Human Member (Part 1)

I'VE INHERITED MY GRANDMOTHER'S MEMBERSHIP IN THE EVIL SECRET SOCIETY OF CATS.
BUT WHAT AM I SUPPOSED TO DO WITH IT?
I GUESS I SHOULD START BY MAKING FRIENDS WITH GRANDMA'S CAT.
HAVE A TREAT, MIKEKO!
WHAP
THIS IS GOING TO BE HARDER THAN I THOUGHT...
ZOOM

Queen: Has concerns about the strange drinks the Doctor makes.
Dr. Meow: Doctor Peppurr.

Notes from a Young Human Member (Part 2)

I'VE INHERITED MY GRAND-MOTHER'S MEMBER-SHIP IN THE EVIL SECRET SOCIETY OF CATS.
MIKEKO, LET'S PLAY~!
I'M STARTING OUT BY MAKING FRIENDS WITH GRANDMA'S CAT.
LOOK! LOOKY HERE! SO MUCH FUN!
YAAAWN...
DEFI-NITELY HARDER THAN I THOUGHT.

Feline Commander: Recruits human members based on information provided by feline members. The initiation ritual is shrouded in mystery.

A Day in the Life of Tanaka

WE NEED TO IMPROVE EFFI-CIENCY.
ADJUST OUR WORK ENVIRON-MENT.
REVITALIZE COMMUNI-CATION.
I'D BE MORE MOTIVATED IF CHATARO-CHAN COULD WORK WITH ME.
WHAT IF WE AL-LOWED PETS IN THE OFFICE?
WE'D NEED TO CONSIDER EMPLOYEES WHO ARE AFRAID OF ANIMALS, AND THOSE WITH ALLERGIES.
BUT WHAT WOULD I DO IF CHATARO-CHAN LAY DOWN ON MY KEY-BOARD ...?
OH, YOU!
CHIEF TANAKA ALWAYS TAKES HIS WORK SO SERI-OUSLY.

Queen: Human members come in all ages, genders, and professions. There are also many other cat organizations with human collaborators and members.

Robocat vs. Feline Commander

TORAE-MON! TORA-TORA!
MEOW.
MEOW.
TORA-CHAN, TIME FOR DIN-DIN.
ROBOCAT CAN RECOG-NIZE AND RESPOND TO HUN-DREDS OF MILLIONS OF VARIANTS ON ITS NAME!
TO-RAZO!
MEOW.
...
THEN WHY HAS ROBOCAT NEVER ANSWERED WHEN I CALLED IT...?
Hey, Robocat!
...

Robocat: Its body is large and looks heavy, but it is surprisingly light and can climb to high places. It demonstrates this function by leaving footprints on the Commander's desk.

Doggoman vs. Feline Commander: The Final Showdown (Part 1)

IT'S TIME TO SETTLE THIS ONCE AND FOR ALL!
THAT'S MY LINE, DOGGO-MAN.
I WON'T LET YOU HURT THE HUMANS ANY-MORE!
FOOL. STOP ME IF YOU CAN.
STONE ROASTED!
ROAST SWEET POTATOES
SWEET POTATOES! GET YOUR SWEET POTATOES!
EAT FASTER! WE WILL CONTINUE THIS FORTH-WITH!

Doggoman: The sweet potato was delicious. Doggoman's Little Sister: So warm and tasty.

Doggoman vs. Feline Commander: The Final Showdown (Part 2)

NOW... ARE YOU READY, DOGGO-MAN?
URP! I SURE AM!
NIISAN, WE NEED TO RUN OUR ERRANDS SOON.
WHAT ?!
ROBOCAT HAS BROKEN YOUR CHAIR, COM-MANDER.
WHAT ?
WE'LL SETTLE THIS NEXT TIME!
YOU BET!

Feline Commander: The Commander's chair has been broken three times since Robocat's creation, and his desk has been broken twice. He now keeps valuable items and photographs in storage.

Secret Society Initiative (Spooky Showers)

WE ARE THE EVIL SECRET SOCIETY OF CATS.
ZSH
WE WILL TEACH HUMANS TO FEAR THE FELINE RACE!
I FEEL LIKE I'M BEING WATCH-ED.
IS THIS SHOWER HAUNTED ...?
WAAAAHH!
UGH! WHAT ARE YOU DOING ?!
QUAKE WITH FEAR, HUMAN!

Dr. Meow: The official story is that when a cat is staring at empty space, it's because their superior ears are picking up sounds inaudible to humans. *Heh heh.*

Hariyama and Kinkuma: A Reunion

SORRY TO DROP IN.
CAFÉ HARI-YAMA, ONE WINTER AFTER-NOON.
IT'S GOOD TO SEE YOU AGAIN, HARIYAMA.
KIN-KUMA-SAN.
I CAN'T BELIEVE YOU'RE RUNNING A CAFÉ NOW.
YOU, WHO WOULD JAB ANYONE AND EVERYONE WITH YOUR QUILLS.
. . .

Hariyama: ... (In my youth, I was as prickly as a pincushion. I couldn't trust anyone. I wandered the streets alone, until Kinkuma-san offered me support.)

Hariyama and Kinkuma: Reminiscence

WE WERE AN UNSTOP-PABLE TEAM BACK THEN.
NO MATTER WHO WE FOUGHT, WE NEVER LOST.
I HAVEN'T CHANGED A BIT, YOU KNOW.
I'LL STUFF EVERY-THING INTO THESE CHEEK POUCHES!
BE IT DOG, CAT, OR EVEN HUMAN!
SEE YA SOON.
. . .

Hariyama: ... (I think Kinkuma-san and I were in similar circumstances. He was like an older brother to me. But after *that*, we went our separate ways. It was...)

Secret Society Initiative (No Towels Shall Be Put Away)

WE ARE THE EVIL SECRET SOCIETY OF CATS.
WE WILL TEACH HUMANS TO FEAR THE FELINE RACE!
PLUNK
LISTEN, HUMAN.
WHEN YOU FOLDED YOUR TOWELS, YOU WERE ACTUALLY MAKING OUR BED.

Dr. Meow: Others worry about his eating habits. Queen: Stop buying Neco Cola in two-liter bottles.

Queen's Stratagem (No Words Needed)

YOU WANT ME TO PET YOU?
OKAY, OKAY. I'LL OPEN THE DOOR.
YOU'RE HUNGRY? OKAY.
SOMETIMES, WORDS ARE SIMPLY NOT NEEDED.

Dr. Meow: Researching the possibility of installing a telepathy function in Robocat. Currently, Robocat expresses its emotions to the Commander with its whole body.

Secret Society Initiative (Cat Hair Teleportation)

WE ARE THE EVIL SECRET SOCIETY OF CATS.

FRESHLY DRY-CLEANED!

WE WILL TEACH HUMANS TO FEAR THE FELINE RACE!

AND I'LL USE THE LINT ROLLER BEFORE I HEAD OUT.

HEAD-TO-TOE CHECK!

YES! MY SUIT IS PRISTINE!

Neko High

CAT HAIR CROSSES TIME AND SPACE TO REACH YOUR CLOTHES!

DANGIT!

Feline Commander: Once tried to grow out his hair to become a long-haired cat. When that didn't work, he tried wearing human wigs. It was a dark time in his history.

78

Queen's Stratagem (All Eyes on Me)

WHAT'S WRONG, KITTY?
MEOW!
CHOMP CHOMP
WE GOOD NOW? CAN I GO?
MEOW!
DO I HAVE TO WATCH YOU EAT?
DOESN'T EVERY-ONE ALWAYS WANT TO BE THE CENTER OF ATTEN-TION?

Robocat: Pulling its tail will activate a secret function, but its owners believe a cat's tail shouldn't be pulled, so the function remains a secret.

Feline Commander vs. Doggoman (Saving Face)

SO LONG, DOGGO-MAN!
STOP, FELINE COM-MANDER!
FLAIL FLAIL
FLAP FLAP
TMP
TRYING TO PLAY IT COOL, HUH?
YAWN

Doggoman's Little Sister: The other day, I got to see the beach for the first time. Doggoman: At the beach, I ran in the sand and played in the waves, and now I want to try surfing.

Secret Society Initiative (Human Stepping Stools)

WE ARE THE EVIL SECRET SOCIETY OF CATS.
WE WILL TEACH HUMANS TO FEAR THE FELINE RACE!
BOING
BOING
WHUMP
!
. . .
BEHOLD! OUR MAGNIFI-CENT PARKOUR!
ZOOM

Doggoman: Has special moves like Doggoman Kick, Doggoman Punch, and Doggoman Tackle, but wishes he could think up cooler names.

Secret Society Initiative (Confusion)

WE ARE THE EVIL SECRET SOCIETY OF CATS.
MEOOOW!
MROOOWL!
WE WILL TEACH HUMANS TO FEAR THE FELINE RACE!
OKAY, OKAY. I'LL OPEN THE DOOR.
. . . ?
CON-FU-SION WILL CLAIM YOU!
PAD

Queen: My owner likes classical music, so I listen to a fair amount of that. Destroyer: She likes historical dramas. Dr. Meow: I like to watch the Commander sing.

The Doctor's Business (Scent Bar)

I UNDERSTAND YOU'VE GOT SOME RARE ONES.
THAT'S RIGHT.
THEY'RE FOR REAL CONNOISSEURS, SO BE PREPARED FOR A HIGH PRICE TAG.
AMAZING... HINTS OF PISTACHIO FROM A TRADITIONAL JAPANESE HOME, AND THE ROBUST LINGERING NOTE OF A FRESHLY DRIED SHIRT.

Dr. Meow: Invented a VR kotatsu, but it got negative reviews for not being warm.

Covert Tactics of the Hamster Gang (The Secret Sunflower Garden)

WHEN A VACANT LOT OR EMBANK-MENT...
SUDDENLY BLOOMS INTO A FIELD OF SUN-FLOWERS ...
IT MAY BE THE WORK OF THE HAMSTER GANG.
THEY USE SUN-FLOWER SEEDS AS CAPITAL, HENCE THE ILLEGAL GROWING RACKET.
QUALITY STUFF.
OF COURSE IT IS.

Hariyama: ... (Kinkuma-san told me that he learned how to grow sunflowers from a certain someone. I remember he had a soft look in his eyes as he spoke. And yet...)

Destroyer's Special Training (Human-Devastating Headbutt)

OW!
WHAM
HEY!
WHAP
LITTLE DO THE HU-MANS KNOW ...
ZWMP
STOP!
BAM
WHAM
THAT THE SOCIETY OFFERS CRASH COURSES ON DEVEL-OPING A POWER HEADBUTT.
WHUMP

Robocat: Robocat has been finely tuned and upgraded by the Doctor. It's rumored to be gradually getting bigger.

Secret Society Initiative (Unknown Cause)

WE ARE THE EVIL SECRET SOCIETY OF CATS.
WE WILL TEACH HUMANS TO FEAR THE FELINE RACE!
SOME-THING SMELLS OFF.
NEED I EXPLAIN... THE CAUSE?

Doggoman: I kind of like my eyebrows.

Doggoman's Little Sister: I want to be cool like my big brother.

Secret Society Initiative (Kittens, Be Giants)

WE ARE THE EVIL SECRET SOCIETY OF CATS.
WE WILL TEACH HUMANS TO FEAR THE FELINE RACE!
OH, THANK GOODNESS YOU'RE EATING!
EAT UP SO YOU CAN GROW BIG AND STRONG!
MAYBE YOU'RE A LITTLE TOO BIG AND STRONG?
WITHOUT KNOWING IT, HUMANS RAISE UP POWERFUL MEMBERS FOR OUR SOCIETY.

Feline Commander: Secretly designs emblems for the Society, and secretly throws them all away. He has yet to come up with one he likes.

Secret Society Initiative (The Fate of Paper Doors)

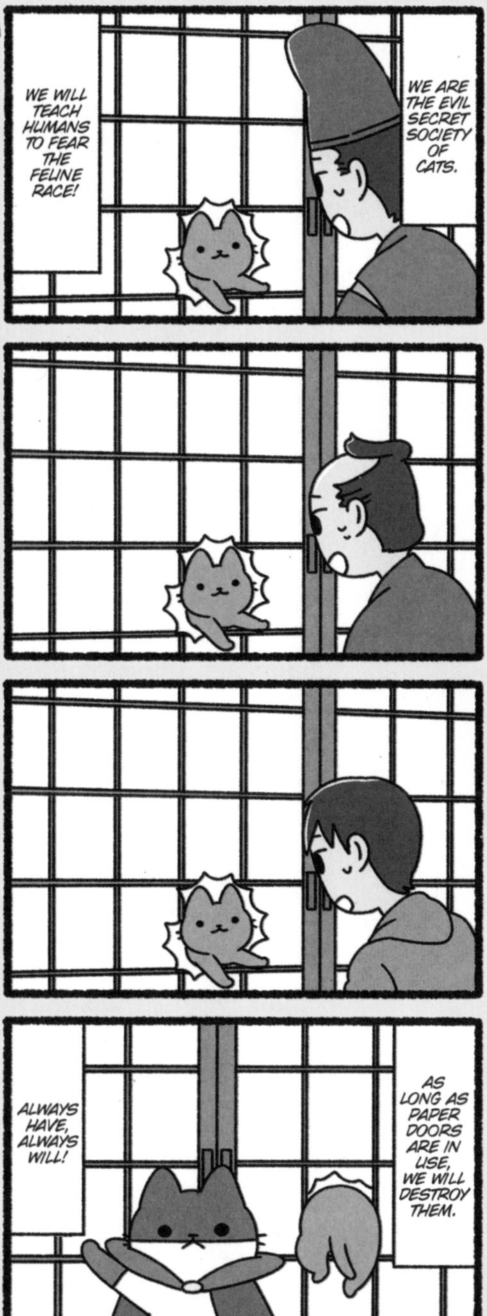
WE ARE THE EVIL SECRET SOCIETY OF CATS.
WE WILL TEACH HUMANS TO FEAR THE FELINE RACE!
AS LONG AS PAPER DOORS ARE IN USE, WE WILL DESTROY THEM.
ALWAYS HAVE, ALWAYS WILL!

Robocat: Was programmed to know that paper doors are made to be destroyed, but its current owners don't have any.

Feline Commander vs. Doggoman and a Child (Part 1)

TODAY YOU MEET YOUR FATE, DOGGOMAN!
FELINE COMMANDER!
WAAAH! MOMMY!
HEY!
WHAT'S WRONG?
I THINK HE'S LOST.
DOCTOR, SEND OUT YOUR DRONES.
ROGER THAT.

Doggoman: Thinks he's bad at card games because of his tail, but hasn't realized that he also has zero poker face.

Feline Commander vs. Doggoman and a Child (Part 2)

DRONE NO. 2 HAS LOCATED THE CHILD'S PARENT.
COM-MENCING GUI-DANCE.
THIS WAY, HUMAN.
WELL, WELL...
HMPH. A HUMAN CHILD'S CRIES ARE HARD ON THE EARS.
STOP IT! DON'T LOOK AT ME LIKE THAT!

Doggoman: I know what Feline Commander said, but he was worried about that boy! I can tell! Feline Commander: Be silent!

Dr. Meow's Cyber Attack

DR. MEOW HAS PUBLISHED AN INTERNET ARTICLE ON HOW TO PHOTOGRAPH CATS.
Take Beautiful Photos with Just a Smartphone
ANY HUMAN WHO READS IT WANTS TO TRY IT OUT.
WHEN THEY GET A GOOD PHOTO, THEY UPLOAD IT.
Likes
#mycat
#squee
THUS, CAT PICTURES WILL GO VIRAL...
AND INCREASE OUR HUMAN MEMBERSHIP!

Feline Commander: When spring comes, Feline Commander leaves the command center and does more field work.

Hamster Gang Code

RATTLE
RATTLE
RATTLE
RATTLE
RATTLE
RATTLE
LITTLE DO THE HU-MANS KNOW…
RATTLE
RATTLE
RATTLE
RATTLE
RATTLE…
THE HAMSTER GANG USES THE WHEELS TO SEND CODED MES-SAGES.
THE SEED DEAL GOES DOWN AT NOON TOMORROW.
GOOD.

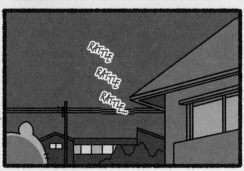

Doggoman: I thought I found a new toy, so I chomped down on it as hard as I could, but it was my owner's massager.

Doggoman's Little Sister: Niisan was so bummed out.

Chief Tanaka's Secret

TO THINK I WOULD FEEL THIS WAY AT MY AGE...
MAYBE I'D JUST BE MAKING TROUBLE IF I SAID ANYTHING.
BUT I CAN'T SUPPRESS THESE FEELINGS ANY LONGER!
TAKEDA-SAN.
I HEARD YOU HOST THE COM-PANY'S CAT CLUB, AND...
YOU WANT TO JOIN?

Hariyama: ... (If we get close, we'll hurt each other with our quills...this was why I distanced myself from others. I was young. But all we had to do was lay down our quills.)

I'D LIKE TO POST ABOUT CHATARO-CHAN IN THE PET SECTION OF THE COMPANY NEWS-LETTER...

SO COULD YOU CHOOSE THREE CUTE PICTURES FOR ME?

WELL, OBVIOUSLY A NAPPING PIC...BUT I WANT TO SHOW OFF HIS PLAYFUL SIDE, TOO.

I CAN'T PASS UP THE FUNNY POSES, AND THAT YAWN THE OTHER DAY WAS THE BEST...

I'M SORRY...

I KNOW IT'S HARD TO DECIDE.

Robocat: Fuel efficiency has improved thanks to a detailed upgrade. Nevertheless, Robocat is eating more of Feline Commander's treats than ever.

Dr. Meow and Doggoman

Homemade Bread
Little Fox Bakery
EGAD! IT'S DR. MEOW.
WHAT IS HE DOING? I'M SURE IT'S SOMETHING EVIL...
SLURRRRP
CHUR
?

Doggoman: I have no idea what Dr. Meow is plotting. Doggoman's Little Sister: (Has never spoken to Dr. Meow.)

Doggoman and His Sister on Patrol

YO, DOG-GOMAN!
HELLO!
YOU'RE AS CHIPPER AS EVER!
AW, LOOKIT THE WHITE PUPPY!
THAT IS ONE CUTE DOG.
FUN SHOPPING. FUN WALKIES.
Shovel Street Shopping Center
THANK YOU VERY MUCH!
SHE'S MY LITTLE SISTER!
. . .

Doggoman: I love meeting all the people in the shopping district! Destroyer: Miraculously, Doggoman's patrols and Destroyer's shopping trips always happen at different times.

Notes of a Young Human Member (Part 3)

I'M A NEW HUMAN MEMBER OF THE SOCIETY WHO INHERITED MEMBER-SHIP FROM MY GRAND-MOTHER.
I'M WORKING HARD TO MAKE FRIENDS WITH MY GRAND-MOTHER'S CAT.
OH! MIKEKO SAT DOWN NEXT TO ME.
I'M SO HAPP--
ACHOO!
WHOOSH
THE PATH TO HUMAN MEM-BERSHIP IS A LONG ONE.

Queen: Both my parents are award-winning cats. I heard they have very long names written on their pedigrees.

Secret Society Initiative (Thwarting Your Decluttering)

WE ARE THE EVIL SECRET SOCIETY OF CATS.
A CLUMP OF CAT HAIR.
WE WILL TEACH HUMANS TO FEAR THE FELINE RACE!
A CLAW.
A WHISKER.
A TOY SHE WON'T PLAY WITH ANY-MORE.
I CAN'T THROW ANY OF THIS AWAY!
TASTE THE FEAR AS THE CLUTTER PILES UP!

Feline Commander: Most recent failure is falling asleep during an online meeting with human members.

Robocat: Appeared behind its owners during a remote work meeting and confused everyone.

Secret Society Initiative (Disrupting Digital and Analog Work Alike)

WE ARE THE EVIL SECRET SOCIETY OF CATS.
Oh no!
WE WILL TEACH HUMANS TO FEAR THE FELINE RACE!
No, no, no!
THAT USED TO HAPPEN ALL THE TIME BEFORE I WENT DIGITAL.
HUH?! I CAN'T FIND MY STYLUS!
ANALOG OR DIGITAL-- NONE OF YOUR WORK IS SAFE FROM US!

Feline Commander: I've grown out of having to sit in any circle drawn on the ground.

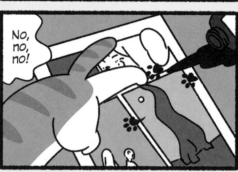

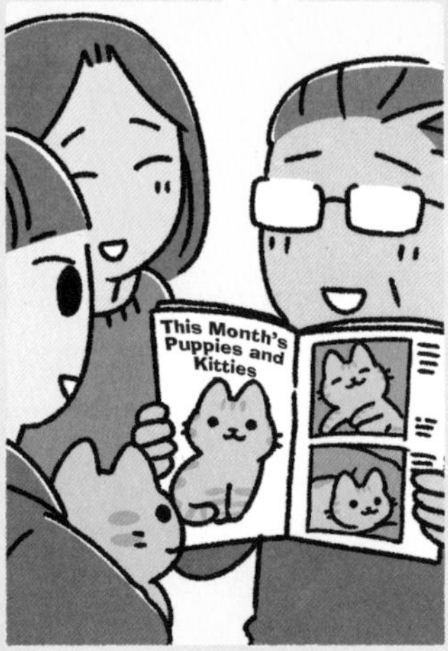
This Month's Puppies and Kitties

Secret Society Initiative (Trial of Love)

WE ARE THE EVIL SECRET SOCIETY OF CATS.
LICK LICK
WE WILL TEACH HUMANS TO FEAR THE FELINE RACE!
LIIICK LIIICK
I KNOW YOU LOVE ME...
LICK LICK LICK
BUT YOUR LOVE HURTS.
LIIICK
LIIICK
THE LOVE OF CATS IS A TRIAL!

Doggoman: I saw a movie where a bunch of heroes teamed up to save the world. I want to make lots of hero friends, too!

Destroyer's Day Off

DESTROYER FIGHTS POWERFUL OPPO- NENTS EVERY DAY FOR THE SOCIETY.
THOSE GUYS YESTER- DAY WERE TOUGH.
I JUST CAN'T SHAKE THIS FATIGUE.
I GUESS THIS IS OKAY ONCE IN A WHILE...

Destroyer: Some things can only be gained through battle.

Secret Society Initiative (Doubt Not)

Panel 1:
WE ARE THE EVIL SECRET SOCIETY OF CATS.

WE WILL TEACH HUMANS TO FEAR THE FELINE RACE!

Panel 2:
I READ IT SOMEWHERE.

Panel 3:
APPARENTLY, WHEN A CAT SHOWS YOU ITS BUTT, IT'S A SIGN OF TRUST.

Panel 4:
IS IT, INDEED?

REALLY?

I HOPE THAT'S ACCURATE.

Dr. Meow: Extraterrestrials, cryptids, supernatural phenomena... So many mysteries in the world, but they're all...heh heh. That's enough for today.

Secret Society Initiative (Strange Events! A Message from the Spirit World?)

WE ARE THE EVIL SECRET SOCIETY OF CATS.
GUESS IT'S TIME I GOT BACK TO WORK.
WE WILL TEACH HUMANS TO FEAR THE FELINE RACE!
HUH ?!
WHAT IS THIS?!
aaaaaaaaa
xdkjvcxjdnnvdc
x,clx,.
xmkiasg
si
IS MY COMPUTER HAUNTED?
TREMBLE IN FEAR, HUMAN!

Doggoman: A hero isn't afraid of anything! Doggoman's Little Sister: ... (Looks like she wants to say something.)

Secret Society Initiative (Super Lucky! Cat Paw Power)

WE ARE THE EVIL SECRET SOCIETY OF CATS.
IT'S NOT LIKE I BELIEVE IT...
WE WILL TEACH HUMANS TO FEAR THE FELINE RACE!
OH, WHAT THE HECK?
PICK UP!
Knight King SSR
Single Summon
HUH? WHAT?! I GOT THE SPECIAL SUPER RARE!
YOU DID THIS!
BOW BEFORE US, HUMAN!

Dr. Meow: There are rumors that he's secretly running a mobile game.

Secret Society Initiative (We Are Immovable)

Panel 1:

WE ARE THE EVIL SECRET SOCIETY OF CATS.

WE WILL TEACH HUMANS TO FEAR THE FELINE RACE!

Panel 2:

I DON'T SUPPOSE YOU'LL GET OFF...

Panel 3:

(no dialogue)

Panel 4:

GUESS I'M WALKING TODAY.

WE CANNOT BE MOVED!

Feline Commander: Our bimonthly bike sitting tournament is a popular event. We have a prize for longest sit and for best pose.

The Doctor's Past (Part 1)

I AM A CAT.
BUT AS OF YET, I HAVE NO NAME.
I WAS CRYING IN A DAMP, GLOOMY PLACE WHEN A HUMAN TOOK ME IN.
MY MASTER WAS A STRANGE ONE.
SOME-TIMES HE SEEMED BUSY BEYOND ALL REASON.
BUT THEN HE WOULD SPEND MONTHS DOING NOTHING.

Destroyer: I don't know the Doctor's past, but I do know those glasses are just for show. Queen: I know he doesn't like washing his lab coats.

The Doctor's Past (Part 2)

IN ADDITION TO THE HANDFUL OF HUMANS WHO WOULD VISIT HIS VAST ESTATE...
HE SOMETIMES HELD LARGE AND NOISY GATHERINGS.
BUT HE SEEMED TO HAVE NO ONE TO CALL "FAMILY."
I was good at making money.
But I feel like I only spent it on trivial things.
So I want you to use the rest for something **meaningful.**

Feline Commander: The Doctor is a Society colleague with magnificent talent! But it is troubling that he tends to break the part of the Society oath that states "sleep as needed."

The Doctor's Past (Part 3)

World Famous Multimillionaire Leaves Fortune to Cat
Cat's Whereabouts Unknown
HEY, DOCTOR!
I'VE COME UP WITH A NEW PLAN!
I'M CALLING A MEETING!
HEH HEH.

Dr. Meow: Occasionally I remember the old days. I'd like to tell him all about the Society's initiatives, the Commander, the other leaders, and the robots. I wonder if he'd find it all meaningful.

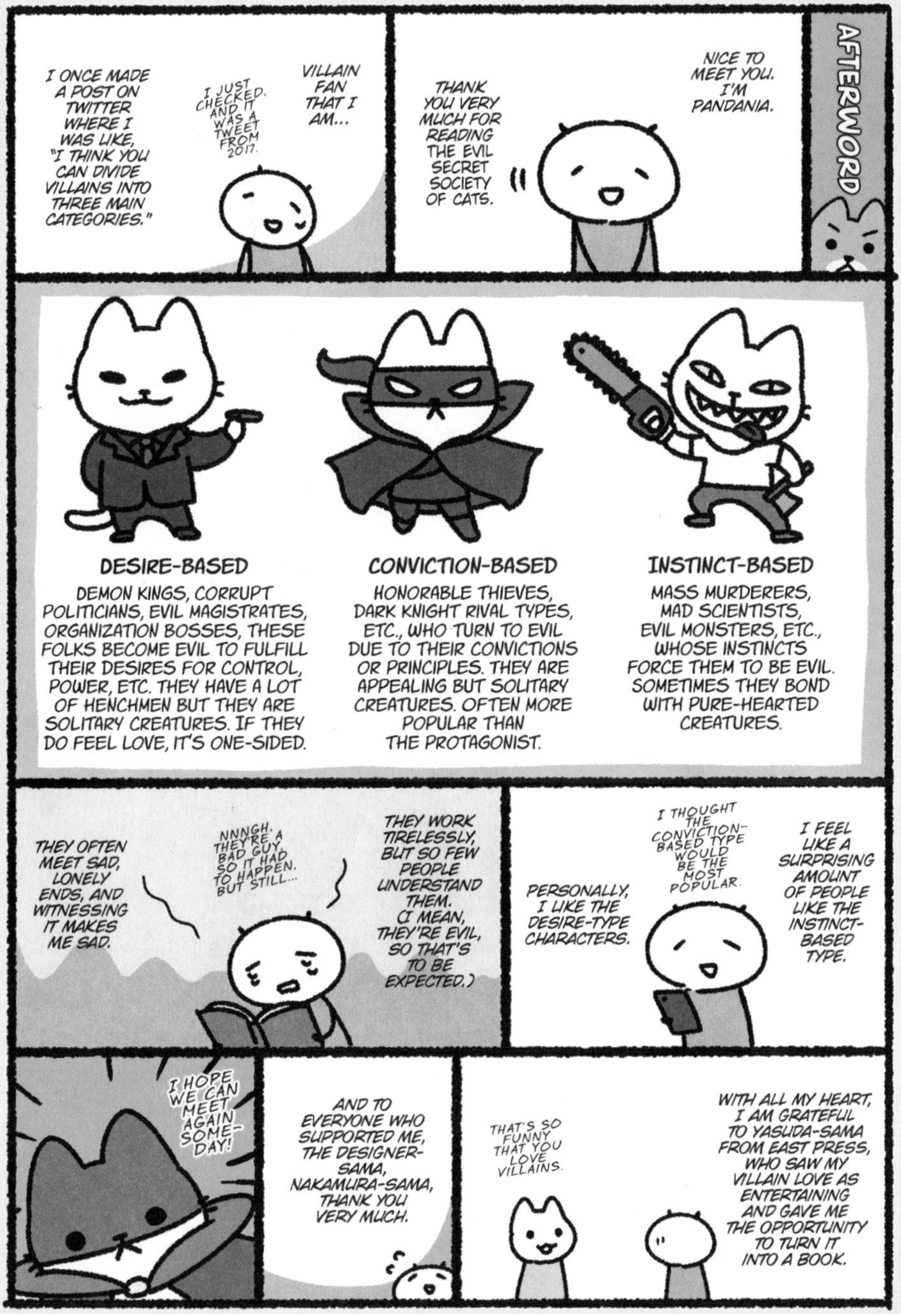
AFTERWORD
NICE TO MEET YOU. I'M PANDANIA.
THANK YOU VERY MUCH FOR READING THE EVIL SECRET SOCIETY OF CATS.
VILLAIN FAN THAT I AM...
I JUST CHECKED. AND IT WAS A TWEET FROM 2017.
I ONCE MADE A POST ON TWITTER WHERE I WAS LIKE, "I THINK YOU CAN DIVIDE VILLAINS INTO THREE MAIN CATEGORIES."
INSTINCT-BASED
MASS MURDERERS, MAD SCIENTISTS, EVIL MONSTERS, ETC., WHOSE INSTINCTS FORCE THEM TO BE EVIL. SOMETIMES THEY BOND WITH PURE-HEARTED CREATURES.
CONVICTION-BASED
HONORABLE THIEVES, DARK KNIGHT RIVAL TYPES, ETC., WHO TURN TO EVIL DUE TO THEIR CONVICTIONS OR PRINCIPLES. THEY ARE APPEALING BUT SOLITARY CREATURES. OFTEN MORE POPULAR THAN THE PROTAGONIST.
DESIRE-BASED
DEMON KINGS, CORRUPT POLITICIANS, EVIL MAGISTRATES, ORGANIZATION BOSSES, THESE FOLKS BECOME EVIL TO FULFILL THEIR DESIRES FOR CONTROL, POWER, ETC. THEY HAVE A LOT OF HENCHMEN BUT THEY ARE SOLITARY CREATURES. IF THEY DO FEEL LOVE, IT'S ONE-SIDED.
I FEEL LIKE A SURPRISING AMOUNT OF PEOPLE LIKE THE INSTINCT-BASED TYPE.
I THOUGHT THE CONVICTION-BASED TYPE WOULD BE THE MOST POPULAR.
PERSONALLY, I LIKE THE DESIRE-TYPE CHARACTERS.
THEY WORK TIRELESSLY, BUT SO FEW PEOPLE UNDERSTAND THEM. (I MEAN, THEY'RE EVIL, SO THAT'S TO BE EXPECTED.)
NNNGH. THEY'RE A BAD GUY, SO IT HAD TO HAPPEN. BUT STILL...
THEY OFTEN MEET SAD, LONELY ENDS, AND WITNESSING IT MAKES ME SAD.
WITH ALL MY HEART, I AM GRATEFUL TO YASUDA-SAMA FROM EAST PRESS, WHO SAW MY VILLAIN LOVE AS ENTERTAINING AND GAVE ME THE OPPORTUNITY TO TURN IT INTO A BOOK.
THAT'S SO FUNNY THAT YOU LOVE VILLAINS.
AND TO EVERYONE WHO SUPPORTED ME, THE DESIGNER-SAMA, NAKAMURA-SAMA, THANK YOU VERY MUCH.
I HOPE WE CAN MEET AGAIN SOMEDAY!

Pandania

Manga artist.
Currently also drawing *Yokai Cats*
(available from Seven Seas).
Cat Folktales (Kadokawa) is on
sale in Japan as well.

THE EVIL SECRET SOCIETY OF CATS

BONUS GALLERY

Here are the illustrations for the graphic novel. Please enjoy them in a larger size.

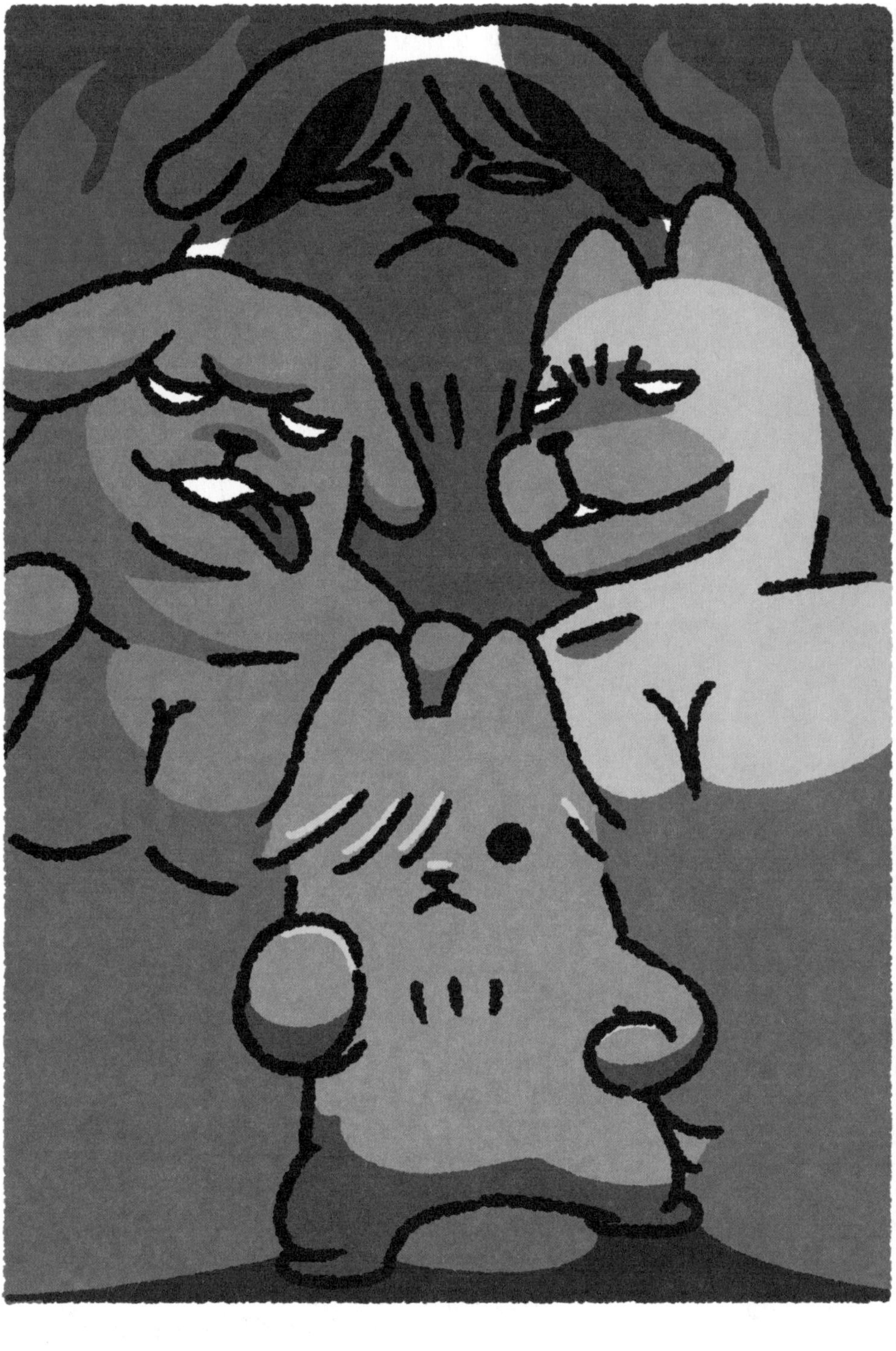

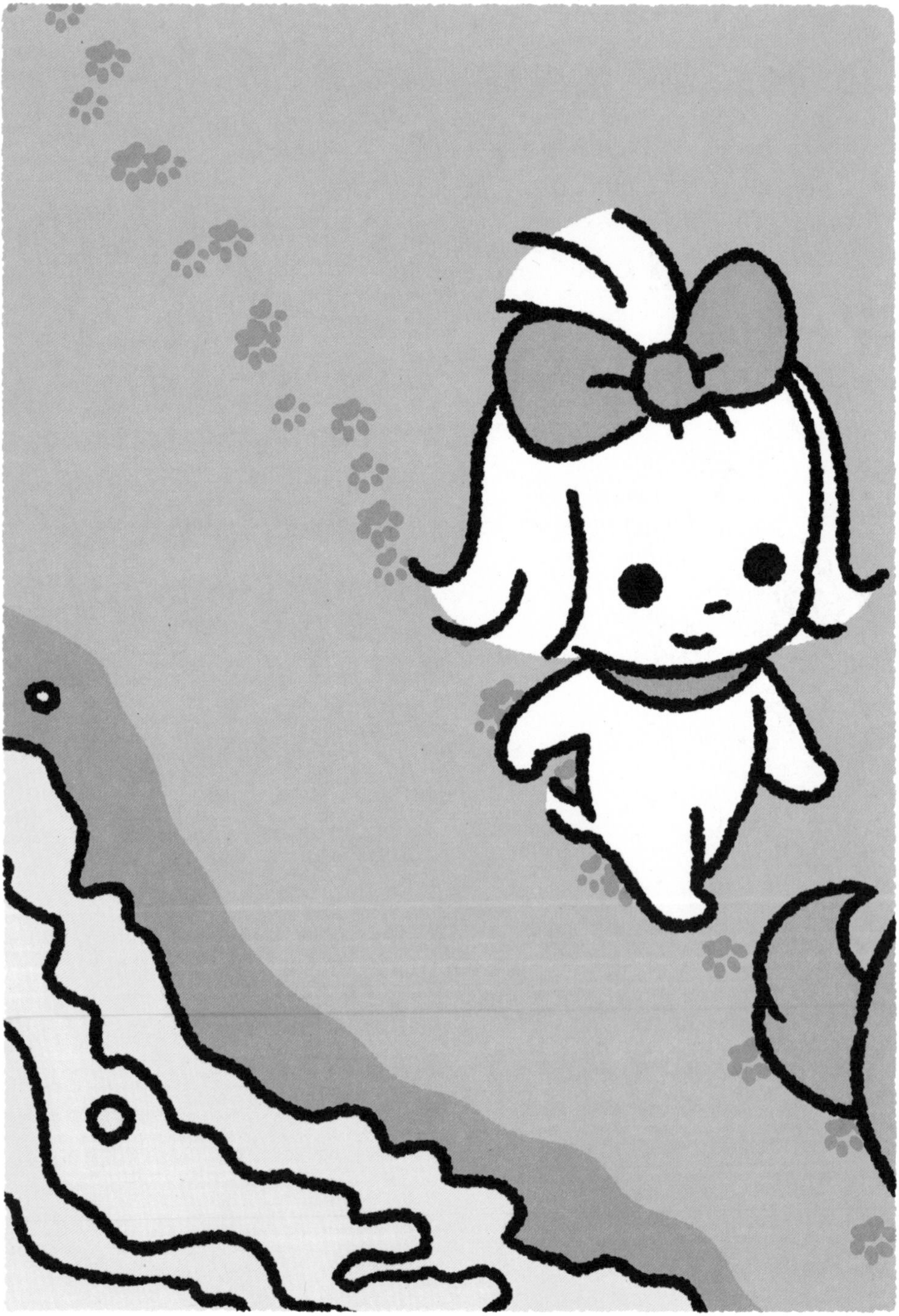

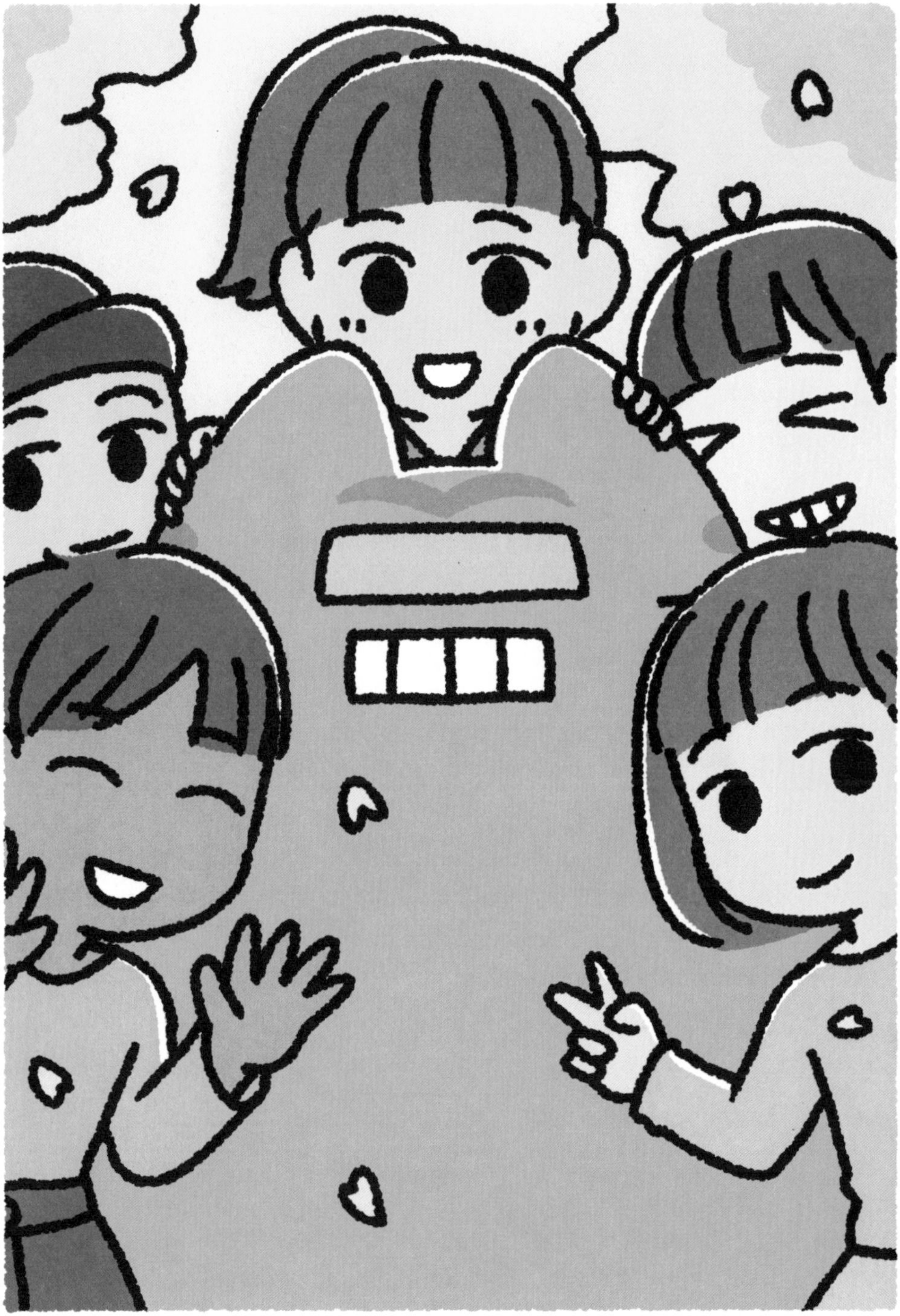

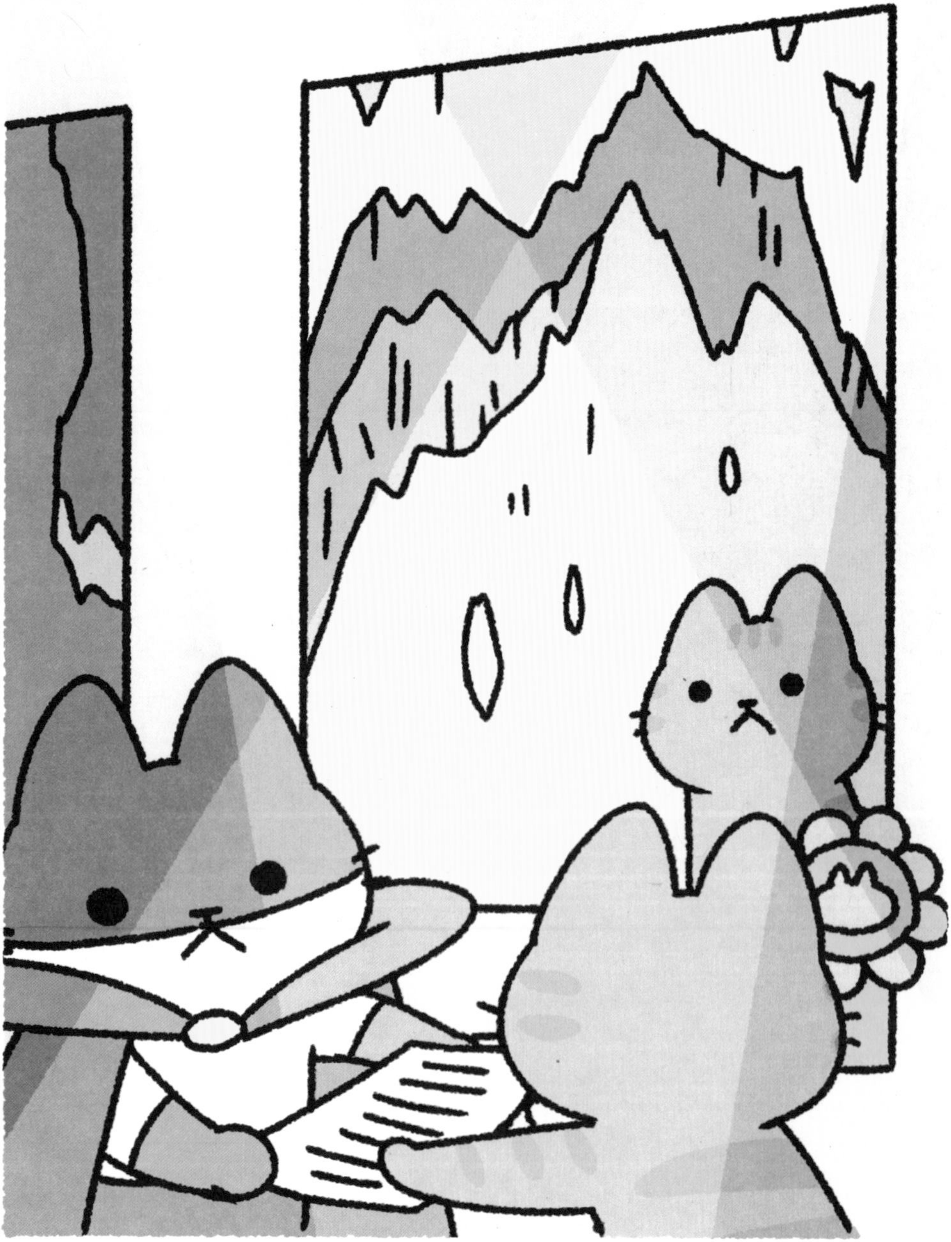

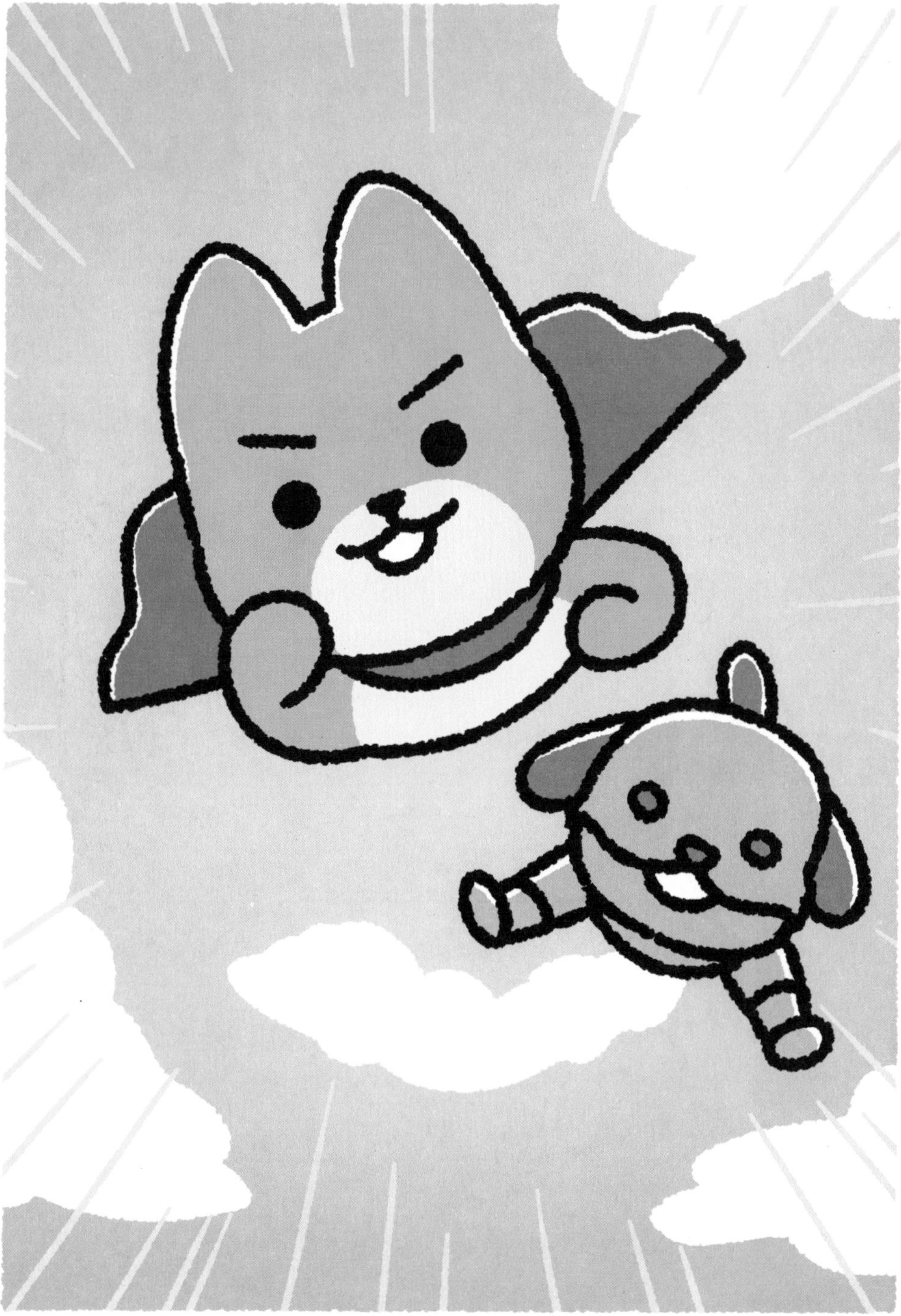

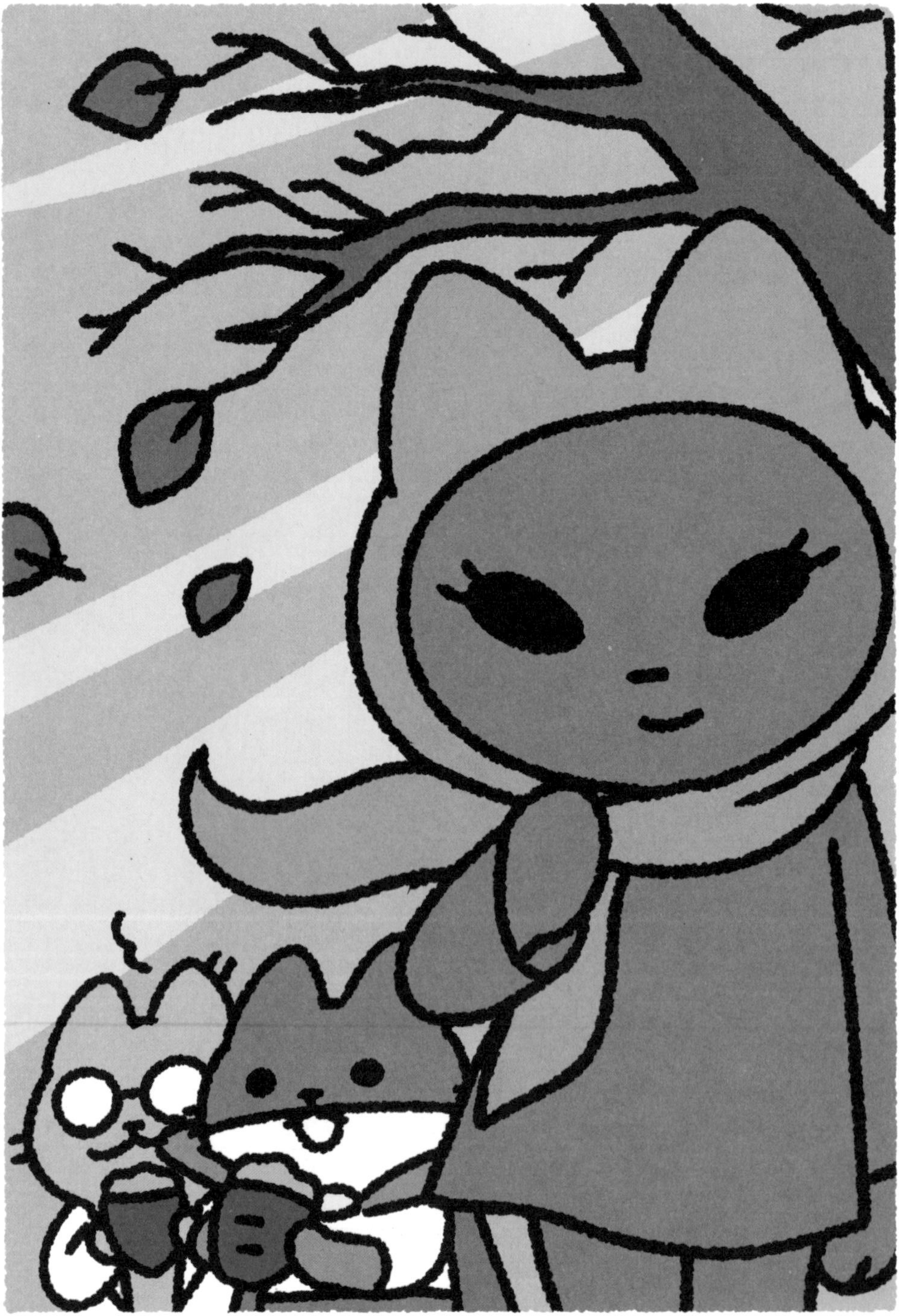

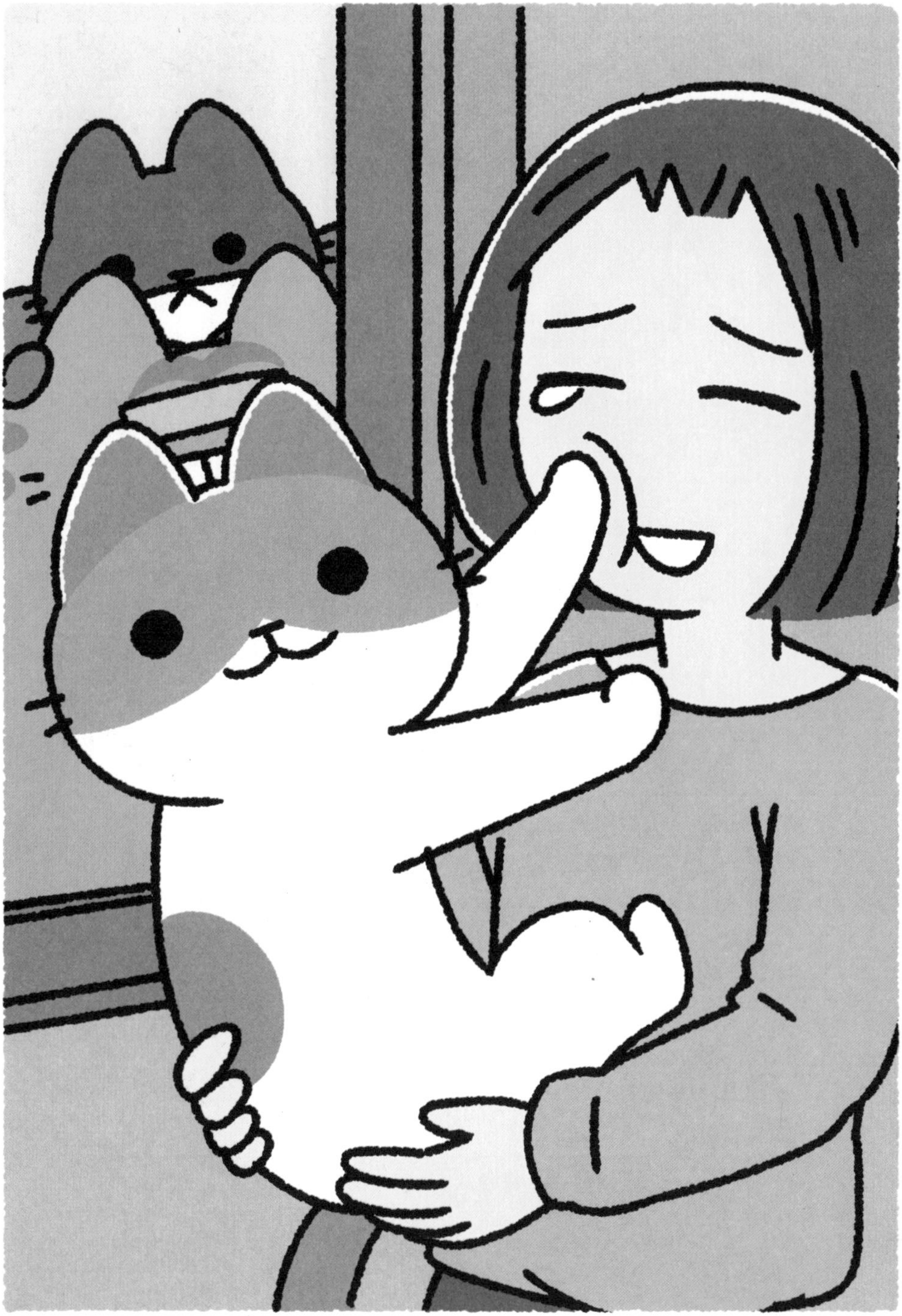

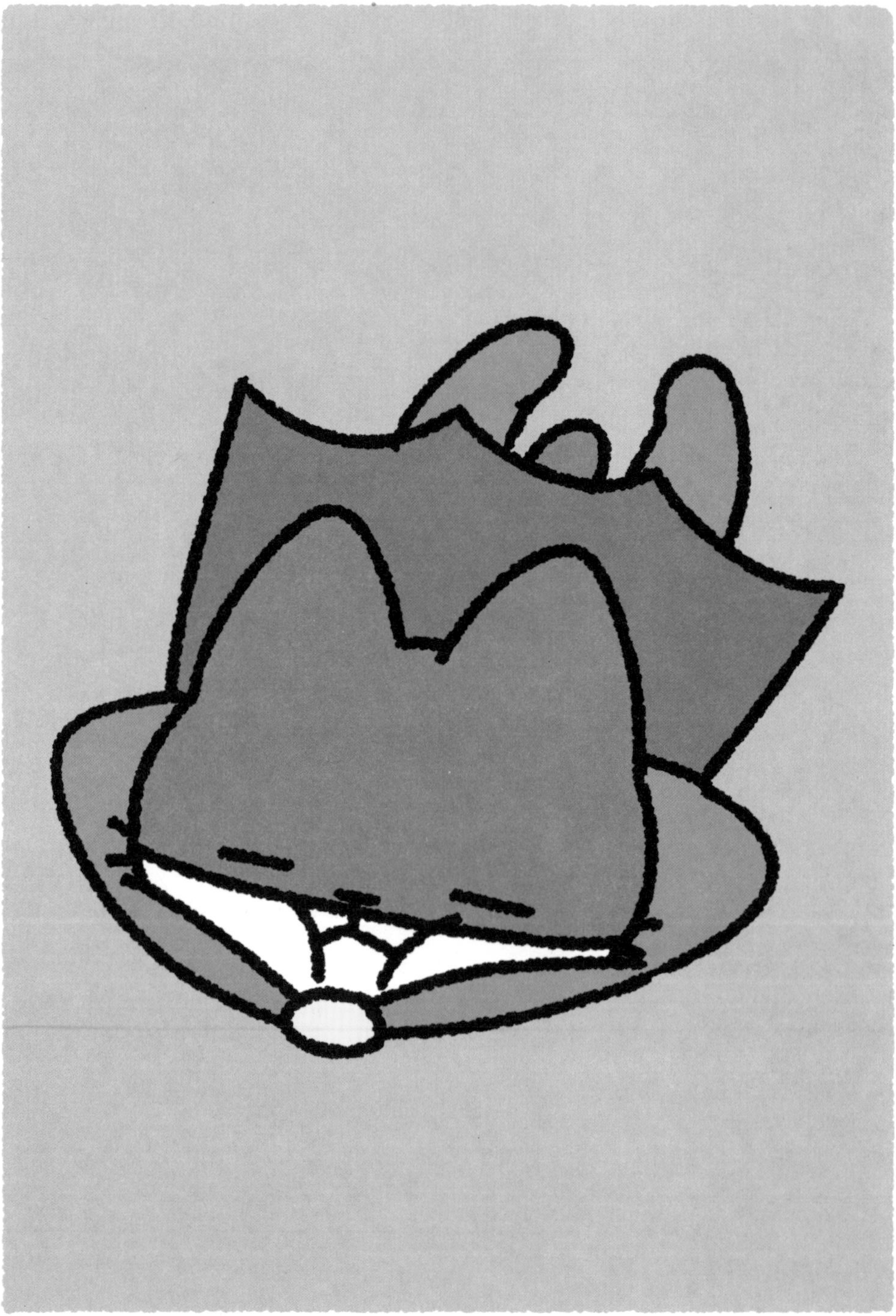

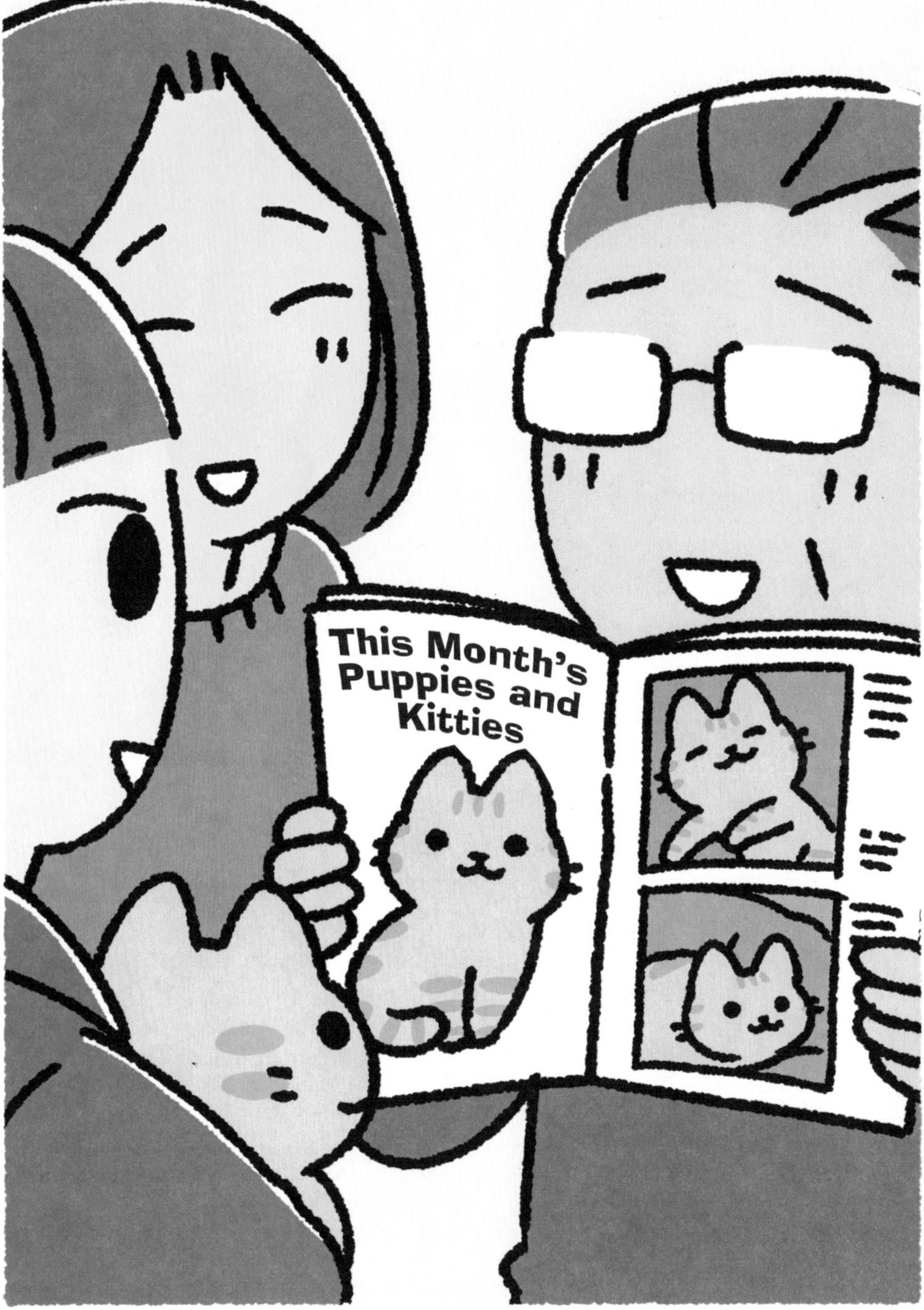
This Month's Puppies and Kitties

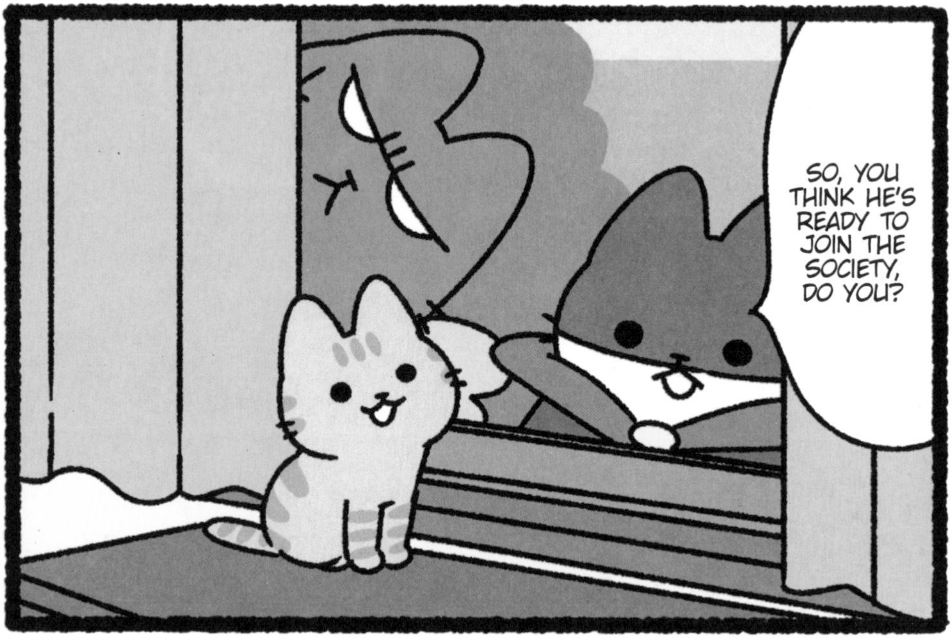
SO, YOU THINK HE'S READY TO JOIN THE SOCIETY, DO YOU?

※Chataro recommends his owner for human membership.

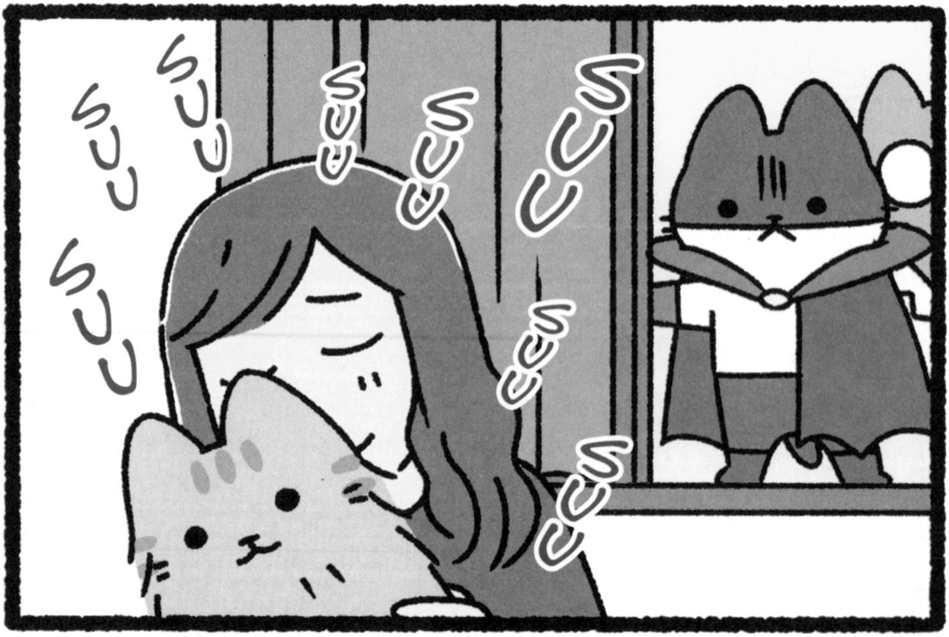
SUU
SUU
SUU
SUU
SUU
SUU
SUU
SUU

※Feline Commander pays a visit to a human member.

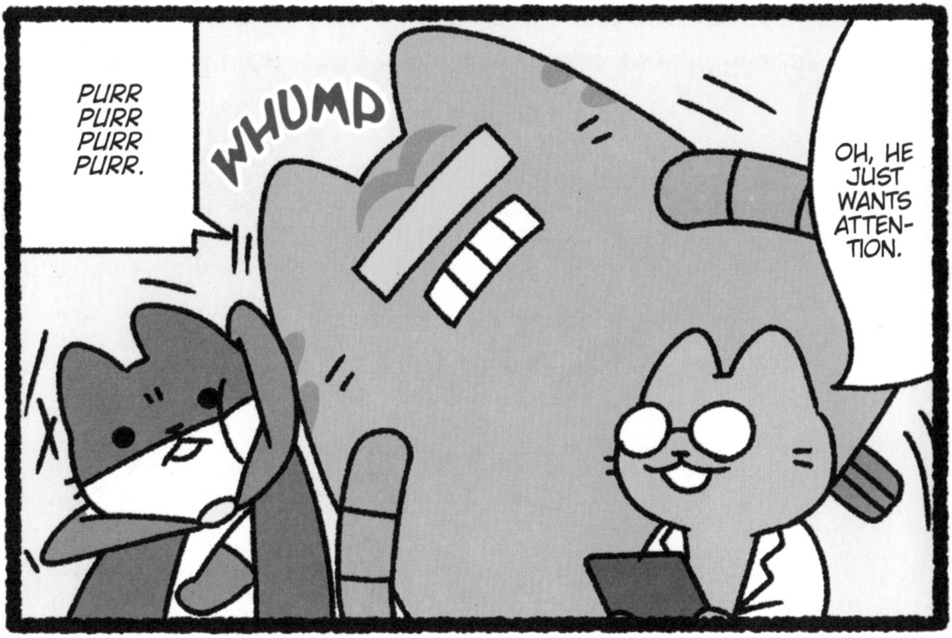
OH, HE JUST WANTS ATTENTION.
WHUMP
PURR PURR PURR PURR.
※Robocat wants attention from Feline Commander.

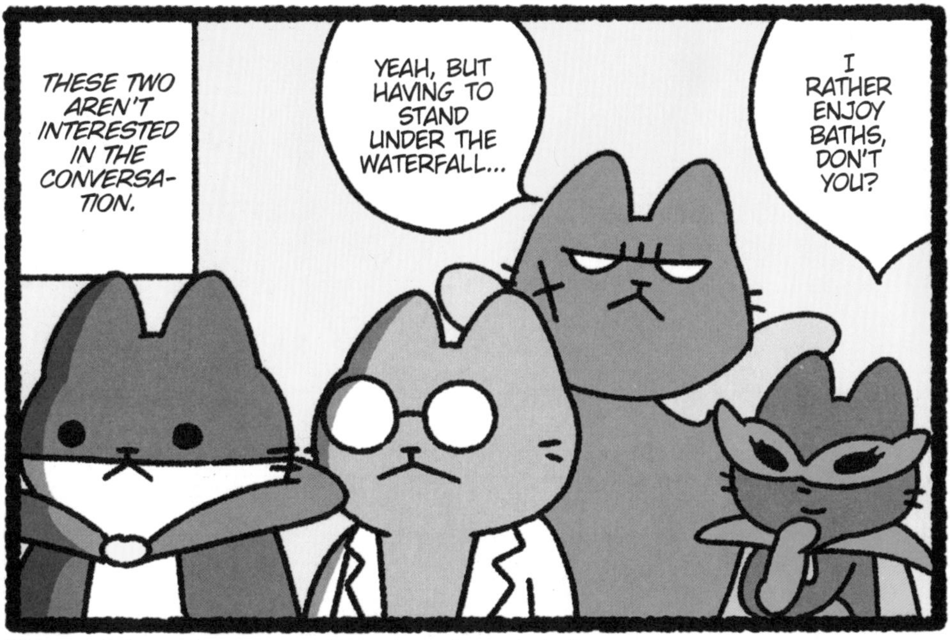
I RATHER ENJOY BATHS, DON'T YOU?
YEAH, BUT HAVING TO STAND UNDER THE WATERFALL...
THESE TWO AREN'T INTERESTED IN THE CONVERSATION.
※Two cats leave the conversation when it turns to baths.

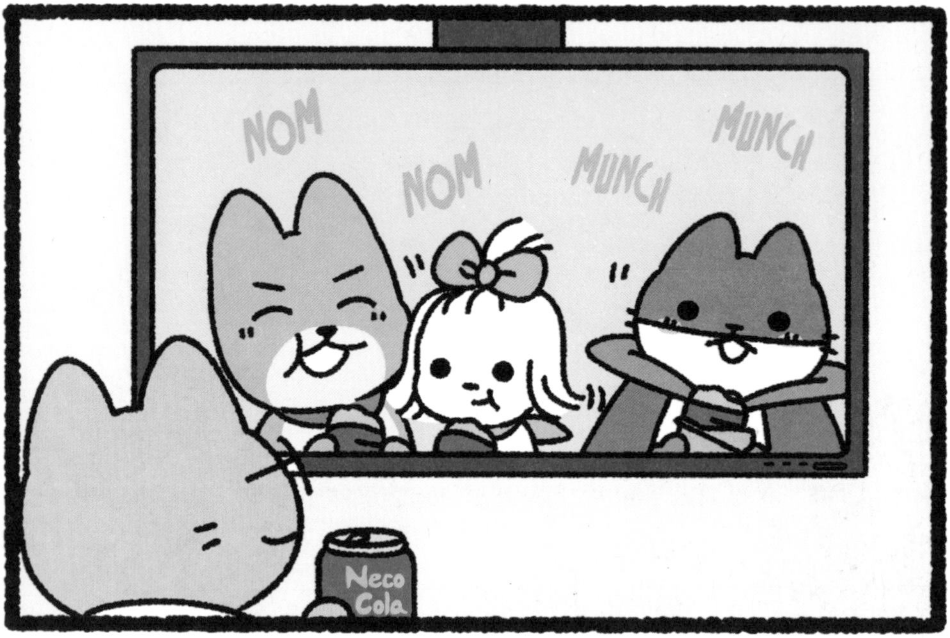
MUNCH
MUNCH
NOM
NOM
Neco Cola

※Dr. Meow analyzes the battle.

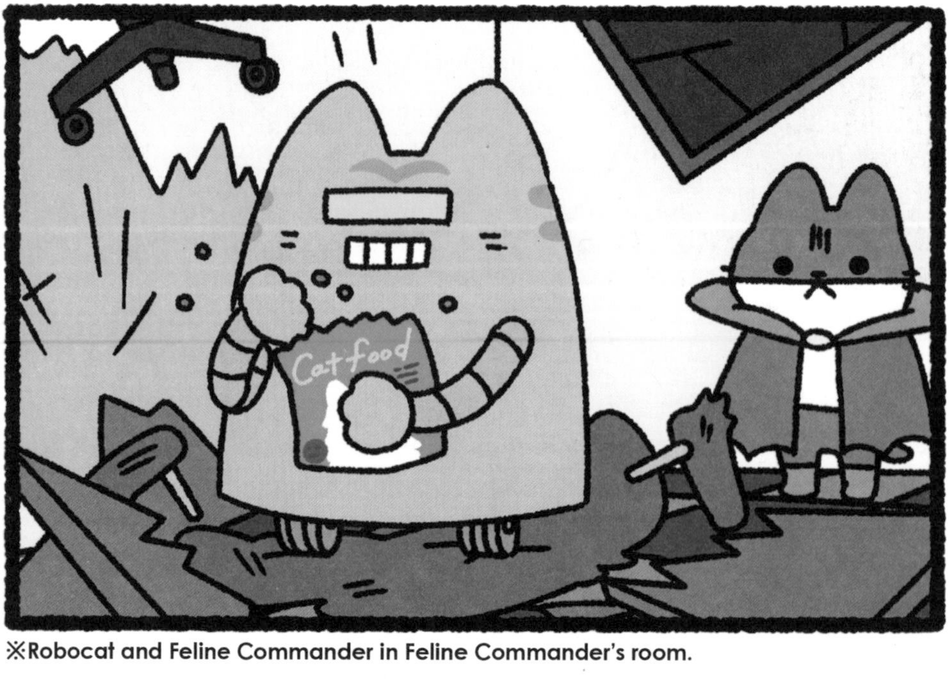
Catfood

※Robocat and Feline Commander in Feline Commander's room.

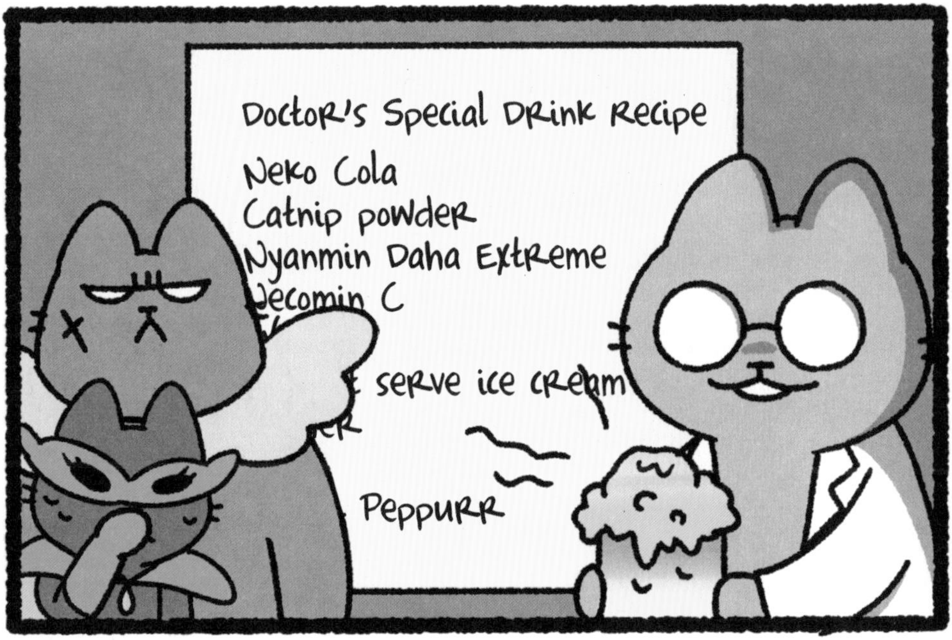
Doctor's Special Drink Recipe
Neko Cola
Catnip powder
Nyanmin Daha Extreme
ecomin C
serve ice cream
Peppurr

※The Doctor's terrifying new recipe.

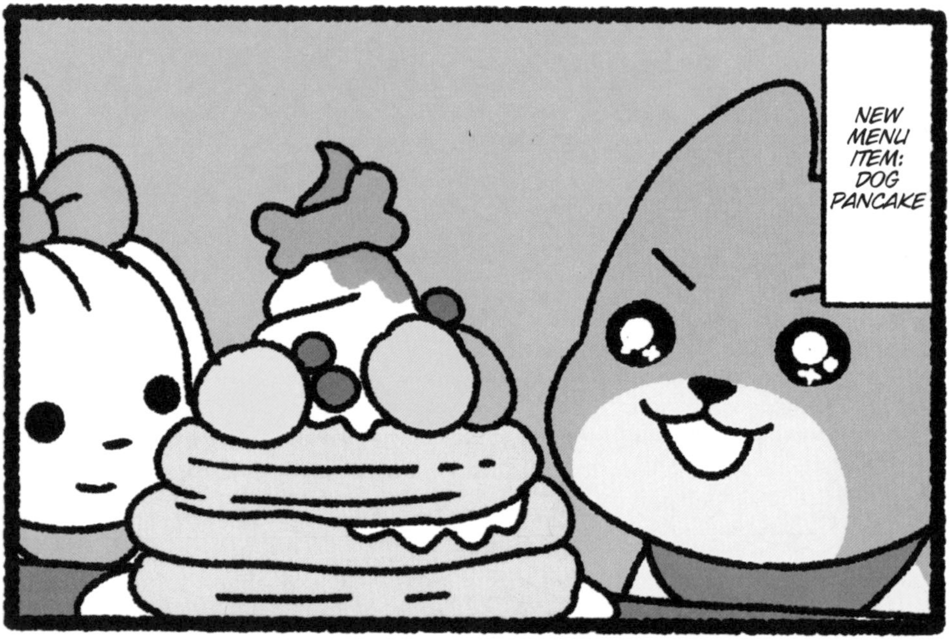
NEW MENU ITEM: DOG PANCAKE

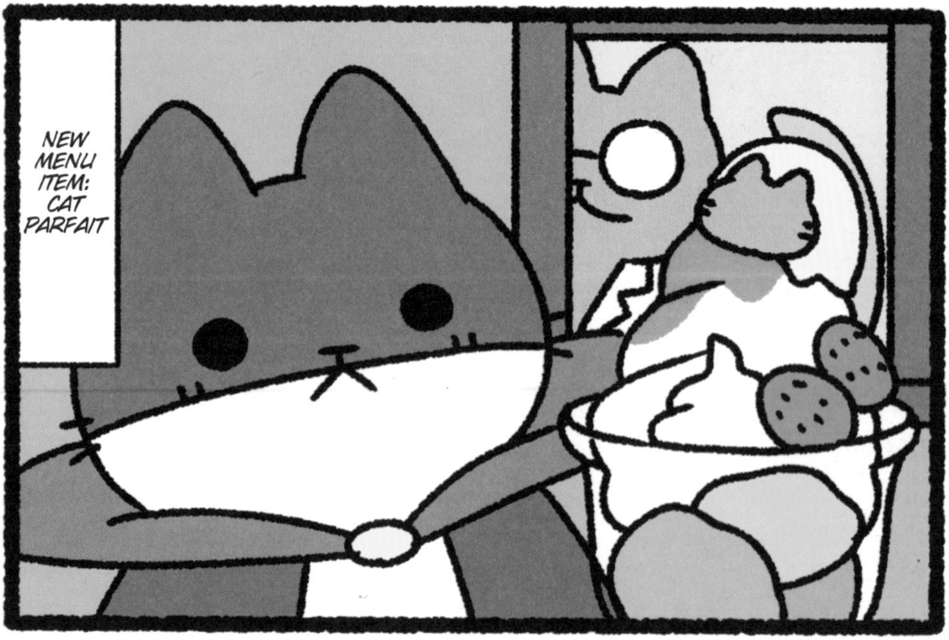
NEW MENU ITEM: CAT PARFAIT

※New additions to Café Hariyama's menu.

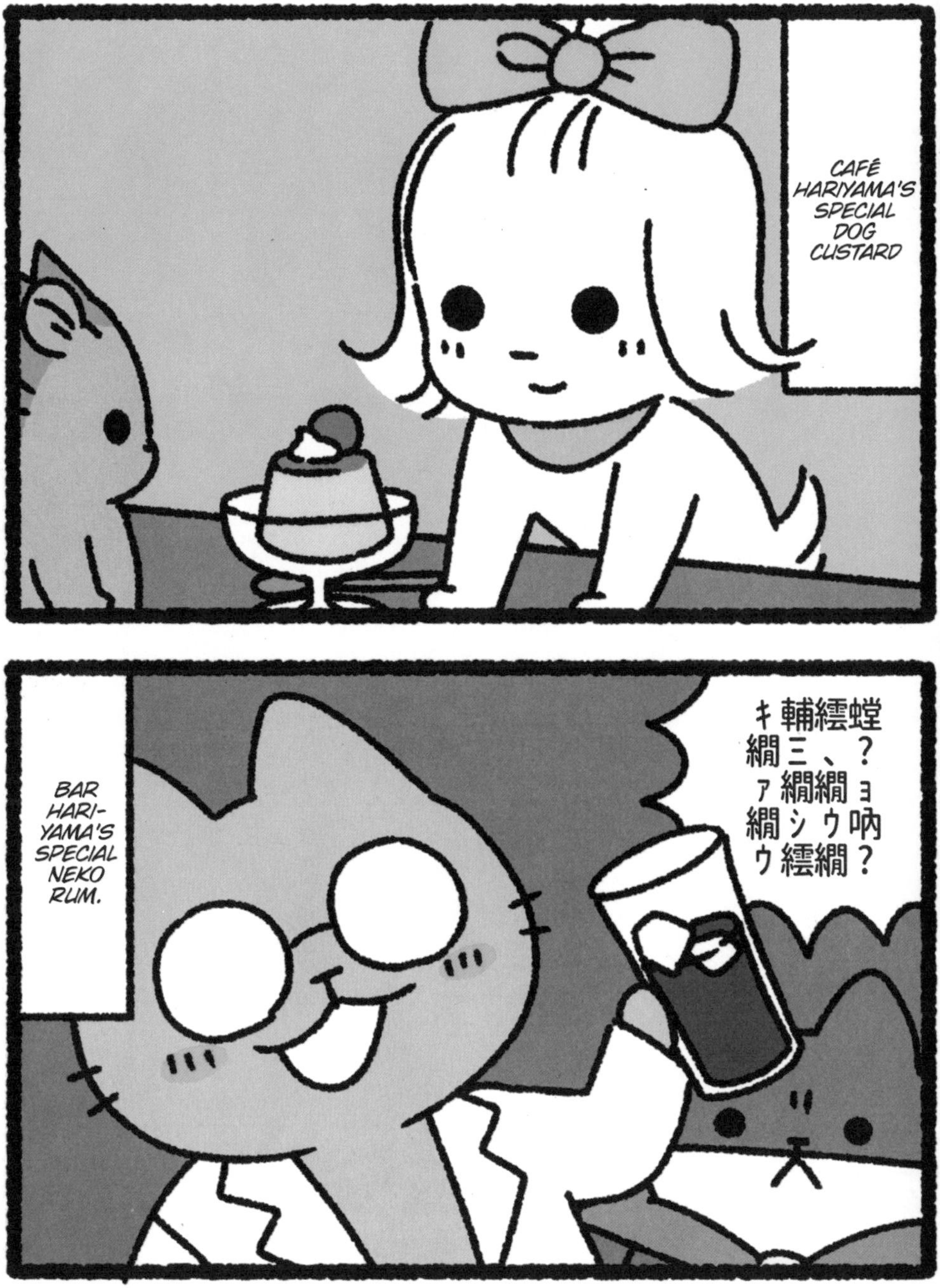
CAFÉ HARIYAMA'S SPECIAL DOG CUSTARD
キ輔繧蝗綢三、？ァ綢綢ョ綢シウ吶ウ繧綢？
BAR HARI-YAMA'S SPECIAL NEKO RUM.

※Popular menu items at Café Hariyama and Bar Hariyama.

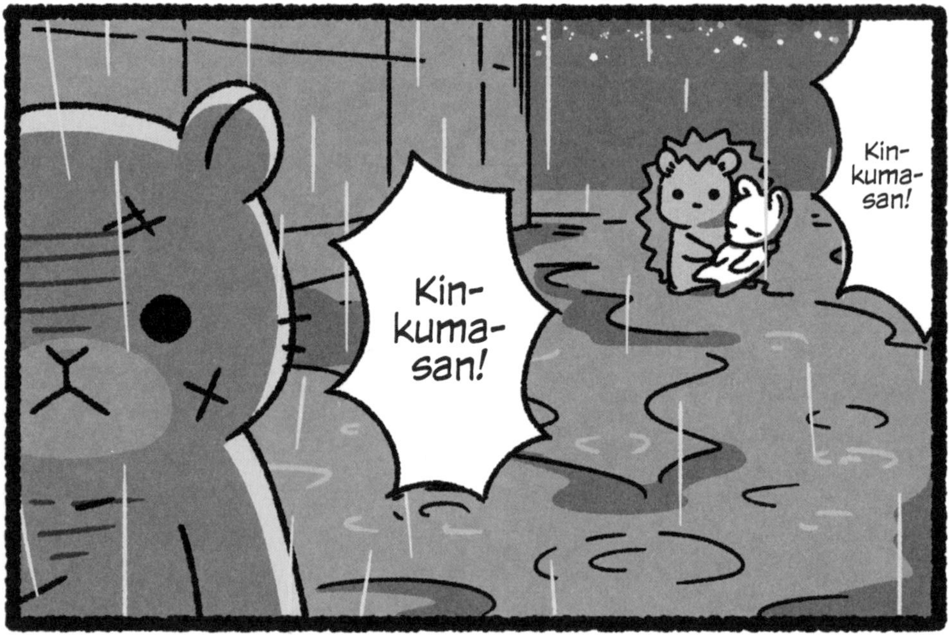
Kin-kuma-san!
Kin-kuma-san!

※Kinkuma and Hariyama's past.

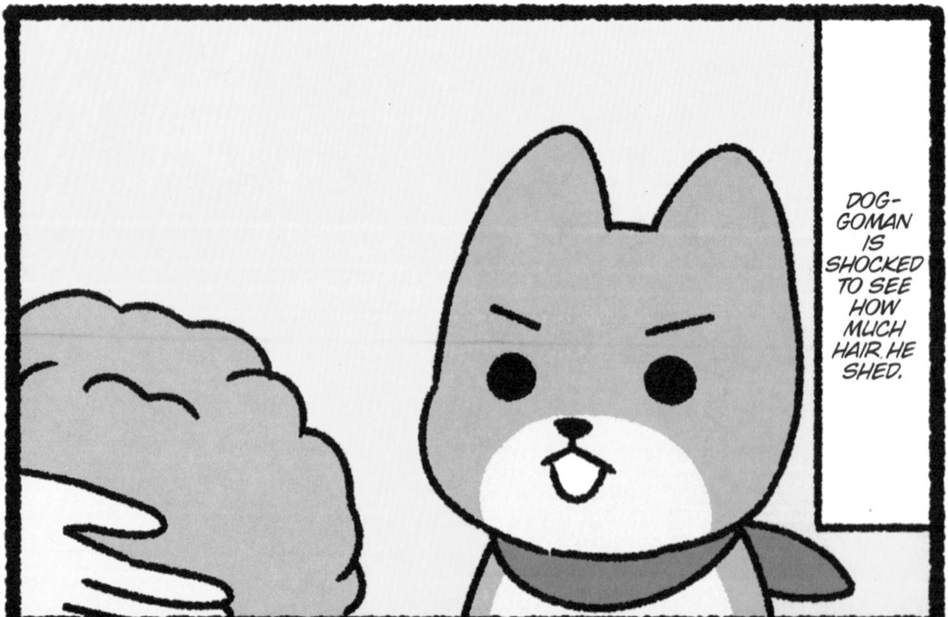
DOG-GOMAN IS SHOCKED TO SEE HOW MUCH HAIR HE SHED.

※Shedding season.

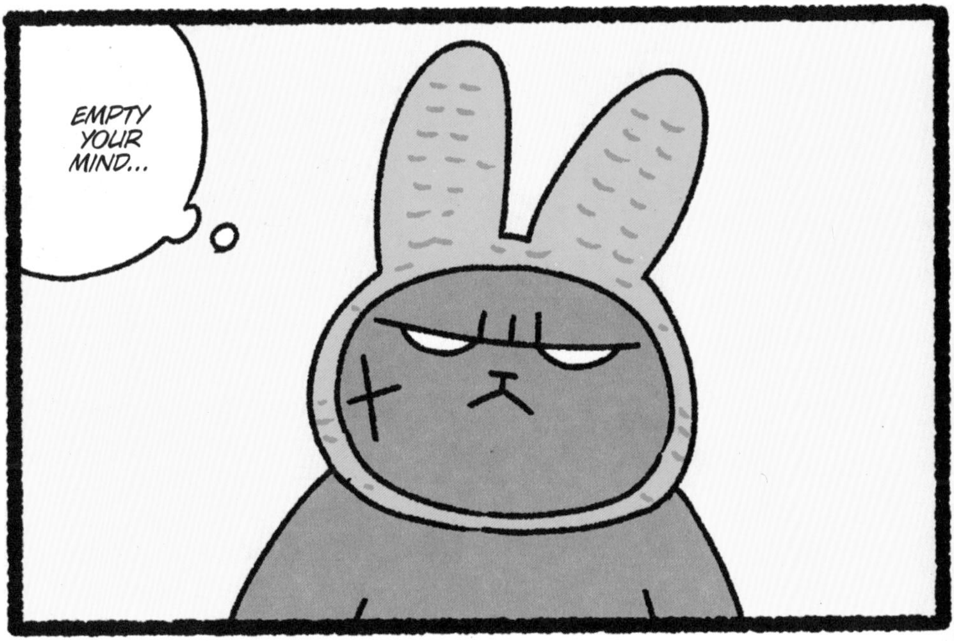
EMPTY YOUR MIND...

※Destroyer puts his training to good use.

Digital Edition Bonus Material: Robocat Cross-Section

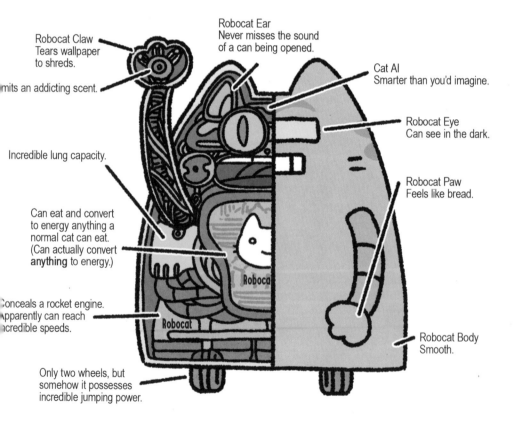

Robocat Claw
Tears wallpaper
to shreds.
mits an addicting scent.
Robocat Ear
Never misses the sound
of a can being opened.
Cat AI
Smarter than you'd imagine.
Robocat Eye
Can see in the dark.
Incredible lung capacity.
Robocat Paw
Feels like bread.
Can eat and convert
to energy anything a
normal cat can eat.
(Can actually convert
anything to energy.)
Roboca
onceals a rocket engine.
pparently can reach
credible speeds.
Robocat
Robocat Body
Smooth.
Only two wheels, but
somehow it possesses
incredible jumping power.

The various poses of cover kitties.

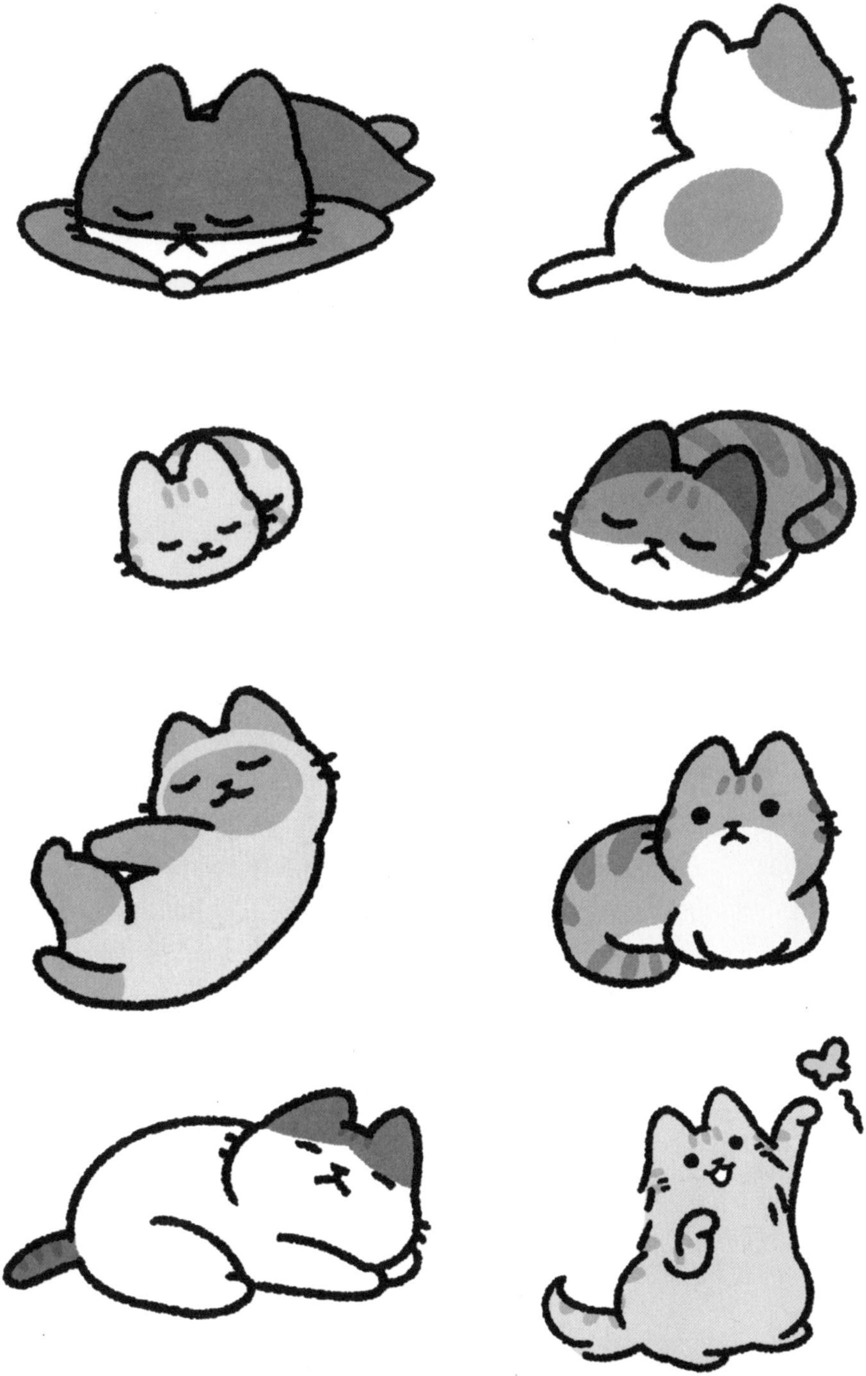

Enjoy these PURRFECT reads from Seven Seas!

Experience all that Seven Seas has to offer at
SEVENSEASENTERTAINMENT.com

SEVEN SEAS ENTERTAINMENT PRESENTS

THE EVIL SECRET SOCIETY OF CATS 2

story & art by PANDANIA

TRANSLATION
Alethea & Athena Nibley

LETTERING
Bambi Eloriaga-Amago
Roland Amago

COVER DESIGN
H. Qi

PROOFREADING
Leighanna DeRouen

SENIOR EDITOR
Shanti Whitesides

PRODUCTION DESIGNER
Christina McKenzie

PRODUCTION MANAGER
Lissa Pattillo

PREPRESS TECHNICIAN
Melanie Ujimori
Jules Valera

EDITOR-IN-CHIEF
Julie Davis

ASSOCIATE PUBLISHER
Adam Arnold

PUBLISHER
Jason DeAngelis

Aku no Himitsukessha Neko
© pandania 2021
Originally published in Japan in 2021 by EAST PRESS CO., LTD., Tokyo.
English translation rights arranged with EAST PRESS CO., LTD., Tokyo,
through TOHAN CORPORATION, Tokyo.

No portion of this book may be reproduced or transmitted in any form without written permission from the copyright holders. This is a work of fiction. Names, characters, places, and incidents are the products of the author's imagination or are used fictitiously. Any resemblance to actual events, locales, or persons, living or dead, is entirely coincidental. Any information or opinions expressed by the creators of this book belong to those individual creators and do not necessarily reflect the views of Seven Seas Entertainment or its employees.

Seven Seas press and purchase enquiries can be sent to Marketing Manager Lianne Sentar at press@gomanga.com. Information regarding the distribution and purchase of digital editions is available from Digital Manager CK Russell at digital@gomanga.com.

Seven Seas and the Seven Seas logo are trademarks of Seven Seas Entertainment. All rights reserved.

ISBN: 978-1-63858-812-2
Printed in Canada
First Printing: January 2023
10 9 8 7 6 5 4 3 2 1

//// READING DIRECTIONS ////

This book reads from *right to left*, Japanese style. If this is your first time reading manga, you start reading from the top right panel on each page and take it from there. If you get lost, just follow the numbered diagram here. It may seem backwards at first, but you'll get the hang of it! Have fun!!

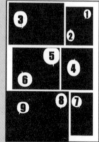

Follow us online: www.SevenSeasEntertainment.com

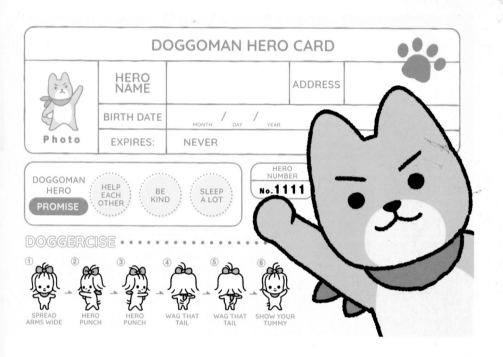

DOGGOMAN HERO CARD

HERO NAME		**ADDRESS**
BIRTH DATE	MONTH / DAY / YEAR	
EXPIRES:	NEVER	

Photo

DOGGOMAN HERO PROMISE
- HELP EACH OTHER
- BE KIND
- SLEEP A LOT

HERO NUMBER No.1111

DOGGERCISE

1. SPREAD ARMS WIDE
2. HERO PUNCH
3. HERO PUNCH
4. WAG THAT TAIL
5. WAG THAT TAIL
6. SHOW YOUR TUMMY

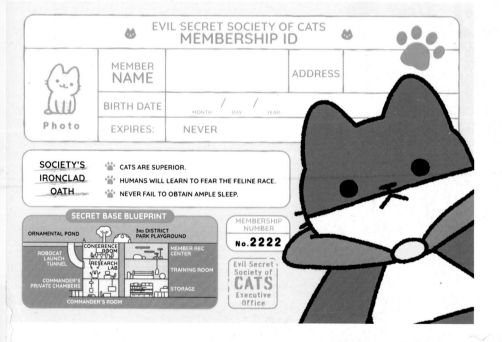

EVIL SECRET SOCIETY OF CATS
MEMBERSHIP ID

MEMBER NAME		**ADDRESS**
BIRTH DATE	MONTH / DAY / YEAR	
EXPIRES:	NEVER	

Photo

SOCIETY'S IRONCLAD OATH
- CATS ARE SUPERIOR.
- HUMANS WILL LEARN TO FEAR THE FELINE RACE.
- NEVER FAIL TO OBTAIN AMPLE SLEEP.

SECRET BASE BLUEPRINT

ORNAMENTAL POND
3RD DISTRICT PARK PLAYGROUND
CONFERENCE ROOM
ROBOCAT LAUNCH TUNNEL
RESEARCH LAB
MEMBER REC CENTER
TRAINING ROOM
COMMANDER'S PRIVATE CHAMBERS
STORAGE
COMMANDER'S ROOM

MEMBERSHIP NUMBER No.2222

Evil Secret Society of CATS Executive Office